A 4 R

gen 9

577

Education and Inquiry

VALUES AND PHILOSOPHICAL INQUIRY
General Editor: D. Z. Phillips

Also in this series

Education and Inquiry

JOHN ANDERSON

Edited by
D. Z. PHILLIPS

Basil Blackwell · Oxford

© John Anderson 1980

First published 1980 by Basil Blackwell Publisher,
5 Alfred Street,
Oxford OX1 4HB, England

British Library Cataloguing in Publication Data

Anderson, John, *b. 1893*
Education and enquiry of the late John
Anderson. – (Values and philosophical inquiry).
1. Education
I. Title II. Phillips, Dewi Zephaniah
III. Series
370'.8   LB880.A/

ISBN 0-631-12531-0

Phototypeset in V.I.P. Bembo by
Western Printing Services Ltd, Bristol
Printed in Great Britain by
Billing and Sons Ltd,
London, Guildford and Worcester

Contents

Acknowledgements

The articles in this collection first appeared as follows: 'Anderson as Educator' by P. H. Partridge and 'Anderson's Theory of Education' by J. Mackie appeared in a special issue of *The Australian Highway* in September, 1958, to mark John Anderson's retirement as Challis Professor of Philosophy in the University of Sydney. 'John Anderson on Education and Academic Freedom' by Eugene Kamenka is a revised version of the article which was published in *Quadrant*, July 1977. The article originated as a public lecture delivered in April 1977 at the University of Sydney as part of the commemoration of the fiftieth anniversary of John Anderson's arrival in Australia to occupy the Challis Chair of Philosophy at Sydney.

The papers 'University Reform' (1935), 'Art and Morality' (1941), 'Education For Democracy?' (1943), 'The Future of Education' (1943), and 'Education and Practicality' (1944), were all first published in the *Australasian Journal of Psychology and Philosophy*. I have provided the titles 'Education For Democracy?' and 'The Future of Education' for what were originally reviews of *Education for Democracy* by J. D. G. Medley and *Universities in Australia* (The Future of Education, No. 5) by Eric Ashby.

'Classicism' was published by the Australian Humanities Research Council in its Fourth Annual Report, 1960. 'Socrates as an Educator' appeared in the *Journal of the Institute of Inspec-*

tors of Schools, N.S.W., 12, 3, Nov. 1930 and 13, 1, June 1931. 'Religion in Education' was published in a collection of ad- dresses with this title by The New Education Fellowship (N.S.W.), July 1943. 'The Place of the Academic in Modern Society' appeared in *Honi Soit*, XXXII, 12, June 16, 1960. The version of the 'Lectures on the Educational Theories of Spencer and Dewey' (1949) was prepared by T. A. Rose and Ruth Walker based on a typed copy of the lecture notes kindly lent to them by Dr R. E. Dowling of the Department of Philosophy, University of New South Wales, Kensington, N.S.W. They are responsible too for the titles of the sub- sections in the lectures. T. A. Rose prepared the Index and helped with the proof reading.

I am grateful to all concerned for their help and co-operation and for their permission to reprint John Anderson's work in this collection.

D.Z.P.

Editorial Preface

It gives me pleasure, for many reasons, to be able to play a small part in bringing about the publication of this collection of essays on education by John Anderson. I was introduced to Anderson's work while an undergraduate by Rush Rhees who had studied with Anderson at the University of Edinburgh before Anderson left for Sydney. Unfortunately, it has taken eleven years to produce this collection.

When I first wrote to A. K. Stout in January 1968, it was with a view to finding out whether there were unpublished papers on ethics and religion by Anderson which might be worth publishing. He kindly put me in touch with Ruth Walker with whom I discussed various possibilities. One of these was the suggestion that, should there be a section on ethics, an introduction to it should be written by W. H. C. Eddy. This led to a fruitful collaboration with Harry Eddy. During this period I was also given valuable advice by A. N. Prior and John Mackie. Despite the enthusiastic reaction to my proposals, progress was slow. In November 1970, Eddy was assuring me that my proposals had not fallen through. The main difficulty was to decide on the contents of a collection. It was not clear whether other collections, for example, one on aesthetics, were being considered. In that event, avoidance of duplication would have been essential. By September 1972 considerable progress had been made. In corresponding with Harry Eddy and Ruth Walker it became clear gradually that the collection should concentrate on education. No doubt the events of the late sixties and early seventies in university life, the common confusions and loss of nerve, influenced my thinking. How valuable a re-emphasising of Anderson's view of education would have been then! Yet, these considerations apart, it also seemed to me that Anderson's observations on education constituted the most impressive body of material not represented in that excellent collection of Anderson's work, *Studies in Empirical Philosophy*. True, 'Classicism' and 'Socrates as an Educator' were reprinted there, but these apart, the essays and lectures in the present collection are brought together for the first time.

In November 1971 Harry Eddy brought to my attention a manuscript of his own. He was strongly of the opinion that, even if I were interested in it, it should not take precedence over Anderson's work. He was faithful to this conviction, but, unfortunately, he was not to see either project through. Increasing illness led to an untimely death in December 1973. It now seemed that the whole enterprise of gathering Anderson's essays had fallen by the wayside. I was happy, with the ready help of Eugene Kamenka, to be able to publish Eddy's book *Understanding Marxism* in this series in 1979.

In October 1977 I decided to try again to publish a collection of John Anderson's papers. The issue of *Quadrant* for the previous July sent to me by David Armstrong, who gave me helpful advice, served to rekindle my enthusiasm. At this time, Alan Olding informed me that a group of Anderson's former students had met with a view to publishing Anderson's work. Alan Olding advised me to get in touch with T. A. Rose at Sydney. This turned out to be excellent advice. Tom Rose informed me that such a group, including Ruth Walker, Jim Baker and himself, had met and were anxious to co-operate with me in every way. This turned out to be the case. I have every reason to be grateful to Tom Rose for the care and industry in all his dealings with me concerning this collection. He first wrote to me in November 1977, so we have worked speedily as well as fruitfully. The question of providing an introduction was resolved most satisfactorily by the readiness of P. H. Partridge, John Mackie and Eugene Kamenka to allow their previously published essays to be used for this purpose, the last having been rewritten for the occasion.

Throughout this last period I have benefited a great deal from discussions with Rush Rhees concerning the papers which should be included in the collection. Nevertheless, the final responsibility for the selection is entirely mine. Throughout the eleven years of uneven negotiations, despite the fact that I have never written to her, I have been aware of Mrs Anderson's lively interest in the efforts to bring together a collection of her husband's work. I am happy that at last these efforts have borne fruit.

Swansea   D. Z. Phillips

Part I

INTRODUCTORY ESSAYS

1

Anderson as Educator

P. H. PARTRIDGE

I shall speak of John Anderson as a teacher, and seek to explain
the reasons for the influence he exerted over his students, the
impact he made upon the intellectual life of his university in
the first decade or so after his arrival in Sydney. That influence
was greatest during the thirties. Anderson arrived in Sydney in
1927, which was also the year in which I entered the university. I intend to dip into my memory to see if I can recollect
what it was in his teaching that caused so many of us to fall
under his sway.

What were the general characteristics of Anderson's teaching which attracted students to him, which caused him to be so
novel and compelling a force in the life of the university during
the early years? I suppose each of his students would want to
speak for himself, and each perhaps would give a different
answer. I can only speak for myself, and, in my own case, I
would place first the search for coherence and comprehensiveness that characterized his teaching. He had retained from his
idealist training the notion of a philosophy as being a system or
a 'position'—the idea that a philosophy provides some fundamental apparatus of understanding and criticism which
illuminates all the fields of inquiry: science, politics, morals,
psychology, art. It is a conception of the nature or role of
philosophy which has since lost standing; nevertheless, it was
his development of this conception in his lectures, writings,
and not least in informal discussion, which helps, I think, to
explain his impact as an educator. I do not want to suggest that

he was not primarily interested in the technical problems of logic and of philosophy proper: this would not be true, and if his philosophical views had not been so original and interesting, his development of them in neighbouring fields would not have been so interesting either. But Anderson certainly believed, and induced his students to believe, that philosophy is not simply another specialism, but that it is, in some sense, the most important of all subjects: in the sense that it gave one a necessary key to the understanding of science, human nature, society and art.

From Anderson, then, we got a sense (it may have been partly an illusory sense, but I won't argue that matter) of the relatedness of the different branches of culture; the idea of a common theoretical or 'critical' approach to the different fields of intellectual creation and discovery. Anderson's philosophy was, from one point of view, a criticism of culture. For that reason, it provided an education of an unusually broad and fundamental kind. It was not merely that he introduced one, as any other cultivated and perceptive teacher might have done, to the important things that were being said and thought in the contemporary world and linked them to the history of thought. Anderson was, of course, no mere expositor, not even merely a critic. He was still very young when he came to Sydney: between 1927 and 1937, he was thinking strenuously, still developing his 'position'. And consequently those of us who studied with him (or later worked with him) had the experience of being associated with a thinker engaged in the work of creating a very impressive intellectual construction. He was hard at it, working over the thought of many writers—Russell, Moore, Alexander, Marx, Freud, and so on—accepting, discarding, modifying, relating, reaching out to take in new territory. This is what made him a great teacher in that decade. He commanded few of the usual arts and skills of the 'good teacher'; he was never popular, spectacular or 'interesting'. But he has been one of the few original and also systematic thinkers who have worked in this country (perhaps, in the field of the humanities, the only one). And his closest pupils at least were in touch, therefore, with an ambitious project of intellectual construction going forward: they could observe at first hand what intellectual creation is like.

'Things fall apart, the centre cannot hold.' At a certain stage the impetus weakened. One explanation may be this: Anderson never could have been wholly satisfied in finding solutions to philosophical problems in the narrower sense. His philosophizing was fed not only by absorption in intellectual exploration or discovery, but also by moral and political passion. In this respect, his mind has never lost the impress of his Hegelian predecessors and his Marxist and socialist teachers. Moral and social criticism, a view of the nature or foundations of culture, are for him an essential object of the philosophical enterprise. It was his idea of a 'fully worked-out position', taking in the various aspects of life and culture, including the moral and political, which in his case fed the intellectual fire. And which, incidentally, attracted to him students of such diverse interests. What he had derived from or built upon Marxism was, for this reason, vital to his whole position. Perhaps, then, it was the re-examination, and ultimately the total rejection, of Marxism which was forced upon him by the course which Communism took in the thirties and forties which halted the forward-moving direction of his thinking, and threw him so much into the posture of intellectual resistance and opposition.

I have been emphasizing 'creative'. Anderson himself has always made a great deal of 'criticism'; he has often identified education with criticism. I must add a separate word about this. Anderson's students learned from the example of his lectures (and, in the thirties, could not have learned this lesson as well from any other teacher) what critical thought is: its power when brought to bear upon fundamental conceptions and beliefs. And what was important was not only his extraordinary single-mindedness and concentration in pursuit of a piece of intellectual analysis and argument; one must remember also the character of his own beliefs. He brought to Sydney a new kind of philosophically-based social criticism. From him one learned that the idols and orthodoxies of social life—the state, religion, patriotism, loyalty, the assumptions and conventions of accepted morality—were neither natural necessities nor matters simply of taste or opinion, but legitimate subjects of philosophical argument. He employed against the pieties of our own time and place the Socratic weapons, the logical examination of meanings and justifications. It seems to be a very simple thing to make a point of; yet I doubt whether anyone had questioned religion or political piety in Sydney in quite that way. The point is not that Anderson's own views were themselves radical and impious; there were other teachers, both earlier and contemporary, who had rejected some of the political and moral orthodoxies: J. F. Bruce, for example, brought to bear in his lectures a brilliant sarcasm against many aspects of religion and the state, and may indeed have had a greater immediate influence upon many students uninterested in coherent argument. What was novel and important in Anderson was his manner of rejecting them: by confronting them with a considered and coherent philosophical position. A philosophical position built from many diverse and transmuted materials: philosophical realism and empiricism, Marxism, Freudian psychology, and material derived from literary sources, writers like Shaw and Wells and Bennett.

Anderson, the critic, was an important influence; yet I feel that often he has been too much identified with criticism. I know that some of his colleagues (some of those, for example, who saw him in action only on university committees) picture him as a critic of almost inhuman acuteness and pertinacity, a corrosive mind, but essentially obstructive and unconstructive. I have heard it asserted that this is the type of mind he created in his students. It is a false picture. For it was from Anderson that many of us learned the excitement of speculation. At his best he had (as I still think) unusual powers of theoretical imagination, a rare capacity for throwing out novel and illuminating ideas; he was a great starter of theoretical hares. And he could do this in almost every field that engaged his interest; in philosophy proper, in ethics, psychology, politics, literary criticism. His theoretical fertility was, in fact, one of his attractions as a teacher. And, as a thinker, he appeared to be most attracted and stimulated by those who had the same temper and capacity—men like Alexander, Vico, Marx, Sorel or Freud.

On the other hand, he was no great scholar; I do not think that he has ever had any particular respect for scholarship as such when not combined with theoretical power. He would probably be content to appropriate to himself Hobbes's arrogant self-justification: if I had read as many books as others have, I would be as foolish as they are. He was fond of saying 'I am like Berkeley—a non-reading philosopher' (pretty hard on Berkeley, and even hard on himself); and I remember his once rejecting my praise of an historian with 'but he's a bloody bookworm!' There was a serious weakness here. Not only in his own work, but even more in the training of students he was preposterously indifferent to the techniques and the craftsmanship of scholarship. But Anderson never does things by half, and he suffers more cruelly than most men from the defects of his qualities. No doubt, like many others, he would have accomplished something less as an original thinker if he had been less self-absorbed and self-enclosed within his own thought. But he has paid a rather heavy price, as I shall suggest.

Undoubtedly he has displayed a great gift of theoretical imagination, although it is a gift he has not fully exploited. His patience and application have not equalled his imagination. He has rarely tried to work out in detail his own theoretical insights or to apply his often exciting intimations of truth to the empirical facts they purport to explain. And thus almost all of his potentially most important work remains as fragments and sketches; and I am not speaking here of the submerged and possibly greater part—the material of several books which is buried in students' lecture notes. Many things have contributed to this sad result (which we hope he will use the years of retirement to retrieve), and one of them is what I have just mentioned: his own intellectual self-sufficiency, his lack of interest in the parallel work of his contemporaries. Such a continuous interest may have provided the stimulus for some further working-out; certainly the absence of this interest has impaired both the quality and the influence of his thought. I do not know why, but, from the time of his arrival in this country, he has not attempted to feed it into the mainstream of international philosophical and social speculation, or during these three decades to replenish it from the stream. And, since Anderson has been an acute and original thinker, the river as well as the tributary has lost something of value.

There are other things as well, strongly-held views and quirks of character. He has always insisted that controversy and polemic are conditions of intellectual or cultural vigour; and he himself has always had an unquenchable appetite for it—though I remember R. C. Mills once describing his brother, the late Professor William Anderson, as the 'argumentative member of the Anderson family.' It cannot be doubted that, as a result of some of the great controversies in which he has taken part, he has influenced the course of intellectual history in Sydney and perhaps further afield. I think this is true of his stand on several occasions on academic freedom; and his sustained polemic against Stalinism in the early thirties and later still against Marxism of any colour deeply affected the political thinking of Sydney students. But Anderson is perhaps wrong on the general question of the functions of polemic; he might claim Russell as a confirming instance, but perhaps after all addiction to polemic or controversy, very much attention to public issues, do not combine well with and assist sustained theoretical path-breaking. It is an arguable point; in any case, Anderson has always held, I think, that participation in political activity is a source of strength to the philosophical thinker.

But much of the controvery he has engaged in has been in the academic politics of his own university. He has given years of his life to the interminable wranglings of academic politics. And this is connected with one of the strangest features of his character. He is as local as a magpie. It would be hard to think of a man of comparable ability who has lived so much immersed in the local scene, and so much enclosed in his own personal circle. The scene being so limited, provincial, remote from the world's intellectual centres, the personal circle so much below him in intellectual calibre, the original thinker in him has clearly been struggling against very heavy odds.

But as a teacher he has striven not only to create a philosophical 'position', as I have explained, but also to create from among his pupils what he calls a 'school'. The 'school', as he sees it, is characterized by its members' adherence to a common position, Anderson's position. He has had his 'school'; the intellectual and emotional relationships with those within his circle, students and others, have been extraordinarily close. This is one of the commonest criticisms of his teaching: it has often been said that he produces too much intellectual uniformity, that he does not encourage independence, that his 'school' exhibits too often the intellectual and emotional peculiarities of a sect. This is much less true now than it may have been in the early thirties, because many of Anderson's students have had time to study in other universities abroad. They can begin the task of bringing his thought into critical relation with the other important work that has been done in philosophy in the last thirty years. But Anderson himself has chosen to devote himself to the building of a local Sydney school; he has exerted influence more by lecturing and by intimate association than by writing; but he has not tried to do what he could easily have done—play a part in the great philosophical world.

As I have already suggested, I think it a great pity. But, no doubt, on this as on all other points, he would not lack an argument to defend himself with. For some reason there comes here to my mind a remark I once heard him make of a colleague who, during the last war, took leave from the university to accept an important wartime appointment. 'Poor —, he believes in sacrificing the interests of his university to those of his country.' It is the kind of joking remark that sticks in the memory because it somehow expresses a whole personality. This one happens to be also the epitome of a political philosophy.

2

Anderson's Theory of Education

J. MACKIE

In education, as in other fields, it is easier at the start to see what Professor Anderson is denying than what he is asserting, and what he opposes is plainer than what he supports. But if we begin by examining his negative views we can work through to the positive ones that underlie them and give them coherence.

Professor Anderson has always rejected the view that it is the function of education so to mould the individual that he fits neatly into his place in society. He denies that vocational training, the development of the abilities required for the doing of a certain job, has in itself any educational value, and he regards the selecting of individuals for the social places for which they are naturally fitted, and the deliberate assigning of them to the corresponding courses of training, as hostile to education. Similarly, he is bitterly opposed to 'moralism', to the assumption that the educator knows how people ought to behave, and that it is a part of education, 'moral education', to impose this morality, by one device or another, upon those who are being educated. In such 'moral education' the pupil merely accepts the customs and conventions of the society in which he lives; he adopts as his own, either imitatively or by undergoing a more forcible 'habituation', the traditional practices and attitudes and beliefs.

What Professor Anderson finds wrong with this is that it is 'uncritical': the pupil who is being trained, vocationally or morally, is taking whatever is socially demanded as being of absolute value; he is not seeing through these demands and understanding them as demands. In the same way Professor Anderson condemns the uncritical acceptance of beliefs, and the dogmatic instruction that is intended to produce this acceptance. The pupil who accepts whatever is widely believed as being the truth has not really learned or understood anything, he has failed to see through these doctrines as *beliefs*, as things that people believe, or to grasp the motives that underlie their believing.

It follows that religious teaching can have no place in education. Whether such teaching is regarded as instruction in religious beliefs, the teaching of doctrines, or as the development of religious habits, the attitude and practice of worship, or as moral education, the encouragement of moral and pious conduct by means of religious stories that in some way support morality, religious teaching in every case asks for uncritical acceptance, for an adherence that precedes understanding. Since he holds, on logical and metaphysical grounds, that there are no religious truths, Professor Anderson maintains that there could not be any genuine, that is, critical, learning of religion, any coming to understand religious truth. But even apart from this view, even if there could be genuine religious learning, it is clear that what is commonly advocated as religious education is not any coming to understand, it is the uncritical acceptance of attitudes and doctrines in advance of understanding. By contrast with this, Professor Anderson would allow religion to enter education only as an object of study: that is, there can be teaching not of religion, but about religion, religion as an historical fact, a social and psychological phenomenon.

Professor Anderson's refusal to allow education to be dominated by the demands or 'needs' of society might suggest an extreme individualism or anarchism. But he is equally opposed to the view that education should be dominated by self-expression, by the ideal of self-development along lines determined by the individual's own desires. Nor does he think of education as the cultivation of a number of separate abilities, to be used as the individual wishes. For this view also would leave education as something indeterminate, with no definite character of its own, a mere collection of bits of training to be put together in the service of some purpose that lies outside education itself.

This, indeed, brings us nearer to the centre of his educational theory. He is rejecting any utilitarian or instrumental view of education, any view that regards education as essentially an instrument, a means to some other purpose, whatever that other purpose may be. As against all such views, Professor Anderson regards education as an activity with positive characteristics of its own. What, then, are these characteristics?

Education is intellectual. But this does not mean that it is merely something applied to the intellect, as other sorts of training may be applied to the emotions or to the body. It means that the core of education is coming to understand, coming to know things in a systematic way. Education is the development of genuine knowledge: it is the coming to see for oneself how things are. Since Professor Anderson's theory of knowledge is empiricist he holds that genuine knowledge is based on observation. Since he is a realist, he insists that what is known is wholly objective, that any subjectivity, any relativity of the supposed object to the observer, is a distortion, a confusion. And since he insists on a single level of existence, denying any transcendent entities, any ultimates from which the empirical world derives its existence or its features, he holds that all knowledge is knowledge of ordinary things in space and time. But this does not mean that he regards learning as the collecting of one isolated item of information after another: on the contrary, he insists that genuine knowledge is systematic, that it studies not sheer particulars, but qualities, seeing things as being of certain kinds and as obeying regular laws; true learning is the discovery of connections, often between things which seem remote from one another when considered from a practical or interested point of view.

Education is critical. At any stage, learning has two aspects. It involves both the understanding of new things in relation to what is known already, and the rejection, in the light of fresh discoveries, of some things that one thought one knew. Hypotheses are both being used and being discarded. At any time our beliefs include errors, and we have to unlearn many things as we go on. And criticism needs to be applied particularly to hypotheses that have become prejudices, explanations that claim to be ultimate and self-evident, to all views that in one way or another set a limit to inquiry or divide inquiry into rigidly separated compartments. Education means the seeing through of pretensions of all kinds, of all doctrines which serve as a smokescreen to protect and further undisclosed demands and policies, whether these are social or 'practical' or religious or arise within the organized pursuit of the sciences themselves.

Education is the finding of a way of life. Understanding is itself systematic, and besides, it is not just one accomplishment among others; it affects the whole life of the educated man. The activities, purposes, and attitudes of the educated man are organized about the principles of understanding and criticism.

Education is a social activity. It is not just by a free, personal choice that one can develop understanding, nor is understanding a possession that will stay put inside its possessor. The critical, intellectual life survives as a social tradition, a 'movement' to which individuals are attracted, and in which they are caught up, and an individual can remain critical only by continuing to communicate intellectually with others, to develop understanding in other people. This view that education is itself a tradition is not at variance with Professor Anderson's denial that the uncritical conformity to traditions is a part of education, for education itself, as a critical tradition, cannot be accepted uncritically.

Professor Anderson's detailed educational views and policies follow from, or can be understood in the light of, these basic principles.

He holds that the typical everyday approach to questions of

educational policy is radically wrong. We ask, of any educational activity or proposal, of each method and of each subject, 'Is it useful?' We try to justify whatever sort of education we support in terms of its results, and we feel that to say that the study of, for example, Latin is useless, would be to condemn it. But Professor Anderson says that we should ask rather, 'Is it educational?' That is, does it contribute in some vital way to what we have sketched as the educated outlook and way of life? It is true, of course, that governments and other organizations will always try to use education for outside purposes, and will judge it by its usefulness; but Professor Anderson holds that for those of us who are interested in education to adopt their criteria is a betrayal of the cause of education. We should not defend education in terms of alien values, but rather attack these alien interests and expose their deficiencies in terms of educational values, showing where they are narrow or obscurantist, where their ideas are confused or fall short of objectivity. Educational policy is not a matter of our choosing to add or substact this or that item, to introduce a useful method or to discard a less useful one: it is a matter of finding out what education itself requires.

If we judge learning from what Professor Anderson calls a practicalist point of view, we are likely to regard education for work and for family life as of primary importance, and to count the more cultural learning as of secondary importance, as being merely education for leisure. But if we reject this whole approach, and think not of education *for* anything, but of education as something with a positive character of its own, we may well reverse the order of importance. Professor Anderson maintains, indeed, that linguistic and literary studies, and especially classical studies, have a central place in education. The study of languages helps us to penetrate the screen of words, to break through the jargons that enshrine conventional notions. Comparison of older ideas with the current ones can undermine and expose what from a contemporary point of view seems self-evident. And running through the history of European culture from the time of the early Greek thinkers there is a tradition of critical thought by which education at the present time can be constantly refreshed and fortified against practicalism and servility.

Professor Anderson opposes much of the educational influence of what goes by the name of psychology, particularly the psychology that goes in for tests and measurements and statistical surveys. By and large, the effect of such work is to bring education down to the level of the average individual, to let the attitudes and the capacities of the mass of people determine what is to be allowed and what is to be valued in education. Education as a specific activity, with its own standards and values, must resist such domination. True learning is not easy and cannot be made easy: it advances only by the overcoming of resistances. And true educational success, the kindling of intellectual interests, the awakening of criticism, cannot be measured by the devices of the psychologist.

On the other hand, the teacher has an important part to play. He has to be both the Socratic questioner, bringing the pupils' thoughts to birth and testing them, stimulating intellectual growth by the raising of problems and difficulties, and also the vehicle by which the tradition of learning hands itself on to the pupil. Not, of course, that learning is an inert object handed over by one person to another; some of the materials of learning may, indeed, be so handed over, but the main thing that the teacher has to hand on is *thinking*, and he can do this only by being a thinker himself, and by bringing the pupil into his own discussion of problems.

It follows from this account of education that the universities have a vital and distinctive role. A university is, more than any other, the social institution which might have education as its special concern, the place where the intellectual way of life might flourish and perpetuate itself, and also the centre from which education might spread out into the rest of society, or at least the base from which it could carry on the struggle against uncritical and philistine tendencies. Consequently Professor Anderson has devoted a great deal of energy to two causes: first, to defending the universities against outside control, against demands that they should modify their standards, their methods, their distinctive contribution in order to supply more exactly whatever 'society'—that is, the dominant or vocal sections of the rest of society—would like them to provide; and secondly, to opposing practicalist and conformist tendencies within the university itself.

To understand this view, we must remember Professor Anderson's pluralist account of society. There is no unified social purpose, no common good, no will of the people which it is the function of all institutions to obey and serve. Society is a scene of conflict, where different interests, different institutions, are constantly in competition with each other. Patriotism, unity, welfare, and so on are just slogans by which a particular dominant or vocal sectional interest tries to gain, and pretends that it has, universal support. In this competitive arena, education and the critical, inquiring way of life have to stand up for themselves, and they have to insist that they are just as real, as practical, as much a positive part of society as any other activities are. They have to resist the attempt that is always being made to reduce them to the status of mere instrumentalities, of mere means to the purposes that try to reserve for themselves the title 'practical'.

The distinction between advocacy and description is a basic one in Professor Anderson's philosophy, but it is sometimes hard to see where this line is to be drawn within his views on education. Nevertheless, it can be drawn. He is not putting forward education as he sees it as something which everyone *ought* to support. He is not merely peddling a persuasive definition. His appeal is to those who *are* caught up by inquiry, who do support the thinking way of life because they are, or are becoming, people of that sort. But in making this appeal, it is necessary for him to mark off what he calls education from other things that are being constantly confused and entangled with it.

3

Anderson on Education and Academic Freedom

EUGENE KAMENKA[1]

We live in the English-speaking, 'developed', world, in a period whose dominant intellectual trends and ideologies, and whose fashionable educational theories and practices, are profoundly hostile to everything that Anderson meant by culture, education and academic freedom. There is a widespread tendency today, especially in allegedly 'progressive' circles, toward rejecting the concepts of culture, civilization and classical periods as 'arrogant', 'subjective', 'élitist', not conducive to universal love and goodwill or to the psychological security of the 'under-privileged'. The trend is to pit the demands of the 'community', of 'humanity', 'democracy' and 'equality', and above all of welfare, both material and psychological, against history and complexity, traditions and institutions, against the recognition of competing interests, social conflicts and social divisions that precede, shape and outlive particular individuals and through which individuals become concrete social persons. The abstract individual, who is nothing, is elevated against everything that stands outside him; the alleged requirements of the present and the future are counterposed, uncritically, against everything that has come before.

[1] What follows is a slightly revised version of a public lecture delivered in the Stephen Roberts Theatre of the University of Sydney on Wednesday, 20 April 1977, as part of the commemoration of the fiftieth anniversary of John Anderson's arrival in Australia to occupy the Challis Chair of Philosophy in the University of Sydney.

For such a view of the world, the past is a lifeless museum, a random collection of bric-à-brac, a storehouse from which we draw items at will, abstracting them from their social and historical context and from the particular kinds of men, women, traditions and institutions that created them. This technique has impoverished our lives and our culture while it appears, superficially, to enrich them. It has substituted an empty sophistication for a genuine immersion in literature, history, philosophy and art and a disordered elevation of unexamined feelings and impressions for a structured and coherent grappling with reality through knowledge and thought. We have retreated from Hegel to Schleiermacher, from Marx to Feuerbach and Fichte, from philosophy to mysticism and love-mongering. We have become *actors* in the bad sense that the word had for the Romans—people capable of assuming the *externals* of *any personality* because they have none of their own.

The thoughtless eclecticism of this position, its inability to present a structured and realistic view of the world or of the human personality, its fundamental confusions, reveal themselves in constant and systematic vacillation between the view that the individual is everything and that he is nothing, that the world is wholly alien and that it exists in us, through us and for us. The elevation of the simple, abstract and undifferentiated individual—of the zero in history—has to be complemented by an elevation of the simple, abstract, undifferentiated and hence unhistorical community, on the theory that multiplying zero by infinity will somehow finally give you one. The elevation of a technical, instrumental view of education—education as training for citizenship, service, or life—calls forth the superficially opposed but actually complementary and equally *un*educated view of education as self-expression and the consequent overvaluing of authenticity, commitment and spontaneity. Behind the more general trend are two extremely powerful ideological illusions common among educators, journalists and other pseudo-intellectuals of the modern age—the elevation of goodwill and understanding as the universal social panacea and the constant, all-embracing extension of levelling, of the attempt to pare away all distinctions of talent, knowledge, interests and responsibility in the cause of social equality. It is thus that much of the contemporary pseudo-culture of the media and the entertainment world is a fantasy-culture, devoted to a belief in instant satisfaction, in the possibility of being all things at once, in the equal value of all opinions and the intrinsic worth of all beliefs simply because they are held, especially if they are held 'sincerely'. The spread of these illusions has been accompanied and facilitated by a frightening debasement of language—a loss of precision, of cultural content, in a deliberate conflation of facts and attitudes. 'Contemporary' educational theories and practices combine to further this debasement.

John Anderson, in his long career as Challis Professor of Philosophy in the University of Sydney, displayed a combination of unflagging logical incisiveness and acuteness, an outstanding sense of coherence and connection and an unusually strong and original capacity for creative theoretical imagination. He taught those who were his students to judge theoretical thinking by the highest standards, to allow no discounts for personal charm or provincial modesty and isolation and to guard against the insidious attractions of the theoretically fashionable and the socially acclaimed. He also taught us to examine ourselves, to pit 'what is the case' against what we would like to be the case, the past against the present, the cosmopolitanism of the wider world—in time and space—against the narrow limitations, the provincialism, of our own. He agreed with Matthew Arnold that to see things clearly you must 'get yourself out of the way'—he stressed that the cultured life, the life of criticism and investigation, is a life of struggle, of enterprise and its consequent uncertainties and insecurities—a life lived in the knowledge that there are no guarantees of rightness or success, that its task is permanent protest, criticism and self-criticism, and its reward that of social and political hostility or exile. The life of prudence and precaution was, for him, a mean and base existence; the search for authority, for comfort and consolation, he saw as fundamentally philistine, opposed to the cultured and creative life, an exemplification of ethical evils. Culture and education did not aim at the guarantee of certainty or at self-satisfaction and did not produce them. They rested on the constant willingness to inquire further; they required intellectual discipline and moral intransigence.

Matthew Arnold, G. K. Chesterton wrote in his introduction to the Everyman edition of Arnold's *Essays in Criticism*, a work for which Anderson had considerable sympathy,

. . . found the window of the English soul opaque with its own purple. The Englishman had painted his own image on the pane so gorgeously that it was practically a dead panel; it had no opening on the world without. He could not see the most obvious and enormous objects outside his own door. The Englishman could not see (for instance) that the French Revolution was a far-reaching, fundamental and most practical and successful change in the whole structure of Europe. He really thought that it was a bloody and futile episode, in weak imitation of an English General Election. The Englishman could not see that the Catholic Church was (at the very least) an immense and enduring Latin civilization, linking us to the lost civilizations of the Mediterranean. He really thought it was a sort of sect. The Englishman could not see that the Franco-Prussian war was the entrance of a new and menacing military age, a terror to England and to all. He really thought it was a little lesson to Louis Napoleon for not reading *The Times*. The most enormous catastrophe was only some kind of symbolic compliment to England. If the sun fell from Heaven it only showed how wise England was in not having much sunshine. If the waters were turned to blood it was only an advertisement for Bass' Ale or Fry's Cocoa. Such was the weak pride of the English then. One cannot say that it is wholly undiscoverable now.
But Arnold made war on it . . .

So did Anderson—in philosophy, in politics and social theory, in ethics and education. A certain Presbyterian intransigence, a Scottish suspicion of things English, of urbanity and self-satisfaction (even though masquerading behind diffidence), no doubt helped. But his attack, as always, was intellectual, theoretical. He pitted Heraclitus against Socrates, Spinoza against Descartes, Kant against Hume, Hegel against Kant, Marx and Vico and Freud and James against Hegel and Mill, and all of them against narrowmindedness, illiberalism and the Priests and Sophists of the past and of our day.

Most of the world does not have at present the kind of arrogant self-confidence, the untroubled contentment with themselves and their ways, that Matthew Arnold combated in the Englishmen of Victorian times. But the strains that go to make up this self-satisfaction are and have long been there. Matthew Arnold's conception of his nation as divided into the Populace, the middle-class Philistines and the aristocratic Barbarians—a conception which Anderson made use of and on which he lectured—is not inapposite to much of the world of Anderson's day or of ours: a world in which Benthamite utilitarianism and the associated philistinism are again strong, and common to both Left and Right in politics, an Australia in which there has been a consistent elevation of the state as a means for guaranteeing and fulfilling material satisfactions and as an engine for the 'improvement' of the populace into the state of philistinism (Public Power, as Sir Keith Hancock put it, in the service of Private Interest), a world in which academies are weak and *style*, in literature, politics and life, is increasingly absent. It would have been only very late in his career that Anderson would have been prepared to regret the absence of a genuinely intellectual conservatism in Australia and other countries, of men able to be a Burke to the Encyclopedists and the French Revolution, and yet know that history would be against them; of men able to play an Arnold to Bentham and the utilitarians, a Vico to Descartes, Bacon, Hobbes, Grotius and Pufendorf. The thrust of his work, however, his commitment to culture and his conception of it, always pointed in that direction. If, in the course of his life, his political sympathies and his political emphases changed, this was not the sclerosis of age, though part of it was the process of intellectual Growing Up, a shedding of romantic illusions about the proletariat and the alleged party of the proletariat and the acquisition of a more complex view of social institutions, traditions and arrangements. He believed, for perhaps a decade after 1926, that the working class could help usher in a society of producers, dedicated to co-operative spontaneity, freedom, creativity and enterprise. By 1943 he had come to the conviction that the working class had opted for security instead of enterprise and could not bring about a revolution in ideas and that socialism stood for planning rather than freedom. His own position was thus no longer 'proletarian' or 'socialist', but a belief in the need for permanent liberal opposition. The change in his views, paralleled in many thinkers of his generation, was due to what I believe to be a correct perception of the changing composition of social forces, of the seriousness of threats coming from new and different quarters. Essentially Anderson was neither of the Party of the Left nor of the Party of the Right; he helped us to see the confusion both in the terms and in what they were commonly affixed to. His own central and abiding commitments were to criticism and investigation, to freethought and creativity, and he knew that this commitment had always been and would always be a stance best maintained in opposition. He was, of course, always a radical, in the sense of going to the root of things and of refusing to accept the conventional or the established simply because it is the conventional or the established. He did, indeed, play Socrates to the Athenians. For many of us, the Philosophy Room in the University of Sydney, where he lectured, haltingly and without rhetoric, nevertheless rang with the timeless accents of that great historic drama, from which so much that is great in Western culture derives. Like Socrates, Anderson taught us to value critical understanding and not individual self-expression, struggle and not 'improvement', excellence and not equality, creativity and not the provision of material or social or psychological security. This put him, from the very beginning, very far indeed from the traditional Left in its central and abiding attitudes and concerns, in its plans and hopes for the future, as opposed to some—but only some—of its protests against the present. James Joyce was not one of *their* heroes; Socrates died at the hands of the people and its representatives and *not* because they misunderstood their own interests, or were misguided. They knew what they hated.

There is, today, something of a revival of interest in Anderson. Unlike this volume, much of it concentrates, according to the vulgar fashion of the times, and perhaps of most times, on the personality of the man rather than on the content of his work, on his opposition to religion, censorship, commercialism, war memorials and the 'established', rather than on his approval of and commitment to objectivity, knowledge and immersion in critical and creative traditions, or on his belief in the proposition that the unexamined life is not worth living and that knowledge requires both hard work and the stripping away of illusions. There is thus, in such a revival, much that at the conscious level he would have been opposed to—a yearning to escape the complexities and irrationalities of the day for the security of associating with men who had a confident and developed view of the world, who spoke with intellectual authority and who could thus provide comfort and consolation, a respectable haven of retreat from the agonies and insecurities of the intellectual life. There is much in such a revival that is even shallower than this—a childish glorying in the record of 'confrontations' with 'authority', unaccompanied by any close study of the intellectual arguments that constitute the confrontation; an attempt to make a man who was above all in his intellectual life not a provincial a part of our provincial history; a false belief that the significance of his work and influence can be grasped by studying his behaviour in a pub and seeing the impact of his doctrines on the behaviour of its frequenters, or that one can become like him simply by opposing the same things as he opposed. But if Anderson was for thirty years to some of the most intelligent products of the University of Sydney who had a philosophical bent *the* outstanding figure in that University, it was because of the content of what he said and not because he loved students, acted the permissive father figure and effectively used rhetoric or its even more debased modern equivalent, the art of teaching and the science of communication. In matters of the intellect, he was tough and not tender, intransigent as opposed to permissive, adult and not immersed in openly seeking the love of the young. Above all, he was not a rhetorician: the contrast between the philosopher and the Sophist—between seeking knowledge and seeking practical ends, including the 'art' of persuasion—was for him of fundamental educational, philosophical and ethical importance.

In these circumstances, it is not surprising that the philosophy of education should have been presented by Anderson to his students as neither the centre nor the *sine qua non* of the process of acquiring education or taking the university seriously. This was so despite the amount of time he devoted, in his public life, to the defence of the educational and the academic against forces inimical to it. The Office for Research into Academic Methods, which my university has instituted, in imitation of many other universities, would have struck him as comic if it did not reveal a sad and dangerous misunderstanding of what *was* the academic and how it was to be extended and developed. When Anderson did talk about the philosophy of education, and lecture on it, it was by way of exposing the malign influence of wider social and philosophical confusions, evident in this area as in ethics and politics generally, and not to be understood in separation from ethics, politics and above all logic and metaphysics. Above all, it was to reject the notion that education was education *for* anything and not an independent and self-sustaining activity, with its own internal policies and traditions; it was to reject flatly and categorically the instrumental view of education, whether as a vehicle for 'self'-development or as training for something else. Education, for him, was, as in Matthew Arnold's definition of culture (which he quotes[2]), 'a stream of fresh and free thought upon our stock notions and habits'; it was an 'introduction to culture'[3] ('in the sense of a critical attachment to the abiding forms of human achievement'[4]); 'the aim of education is to give an account of things, to find out *the reason why*, and thus put knowledge in the place of opinion.'[5] But education is also *the finding of a way of life* as contrasted with the mere acquisition of a number of arts and accomplishments'[6]; it depends on the power of the intellect and not on habit; it begins, as Socrates did, with 'the awakening of the mind to the need for criticism, to the uncertainty of the principles by which it supposed itself to be guided'[7]; it involves leading the pupil to exercise critical freethought, to frame hypotheses and test them, and not merely to learn by rote or to parrot authority. It thus differs, quite fundamentally, from instruction, which is characteristic of training. But learning, for Anderson, is a structured process, requiring apprenticeship, ordered study, a systematic building up of information and critical ability through guided transitions from the comparatively simple, linked with the child's experiences and capacities, to the more complex, presupposing greater experience and prior knowledge. It also requires a grasp of specific subjects or disciplines and the skills and habits of mind they develop—the linguistic and literary, the historical and, pervading all of them, the philosophical. Anderson's strong opposition, in his early (1931) article on 'Socrates as an Educator', to the Sophistic process of instruction, as opposed to the Socratic dialectic

[2] In 'Classicism' (1960); see p. 46 in this collection.
[3] John Anderson, 'Education and Practicality' (1944); see p. 157.
[4] Ibid.
[5] John Anderson, 'Socrates as an Educator' (1931); see p. 70.
[6] Ibid., p. 72.
[7] Ibid., p. 69.

which awakens the mind to understanding by questioning, does have to be combined with his recognition that learning is an ordered process, that the Socratic questioning is neither haphazard nor devoid of content, that it breaks up problems into constituent parts, conveys information, brings out alternatives, imposes a sequence and points out implications. The demonstration purportedly accomplished in the *Meno*, after all, is a fraud; the child has not assimilated the truths of geometry in another existence or drawn them out of itself; it is *not* its own educator. The relative weight to be given to spontaneity and external guidance, the ordering of learning by those who know the next step, are matters dictated by the requirements of learning itself and modified by the practical conditions under which it takes place, but to counterpose spontaneity and external guidance as irreconcilable opposites, as I believe Anderson would have agreed, is to take an episodic, Fourierist, romantic view of spontaneity, to treat curiosity as incapable of sustained interest and of appreciating the need for external help. And since, as Anderson insisted, the mind is not a *tabula rasa*, the child not a set of infinite 'potentialities', we judge the child as well as the educator by the results of its schooling, the student as well as the university by his performance in it. But helping the student to understand, for Anderson as theoretician, always involves teacher and student studying together, exchanging doubts and ideas; it does not mean 'giving' the student 'the correct' conclusions. Those who study only what is 'correct', he wrote in his address on 'Religion in Education' (1943), 'are not studying'.

Anderson did not believe, any more than I believe, that the life of sustained freethought and critical inquiry, of logical argument and scientific investigation based on a trained and disciplined desire to know, is a life that every human being 'really' seeks or will find himself capable of. The educational interest, the interest in culture, the immersion in criticism and inquiry, is, like all interests, a *special* interest, competing with others, never succeeding in 'catching up' a whole person or a whole society. Specific human natures and human societies are economies of conflicting motives, interests, traditions and ways of life—there is no total or common human or social interest, no ultimate end in which all distinctions are over-come, all conflicts resolved, all ends shown to be means to a greater or more fundamental end.

Culture . . . is only one force in society [and] it is confronted not merely by antagonism but by a widespread indifference. It is, of course, possible here to exaggerate divergences and overlook affinities. But at least it should be clear that education . . . on the one hand will never be the whole activity of 'educational' institutions and on the other hand operates vigorously outside them. The liberal will still endeavour to make them as far as possible an avenue to culture, a means of detaching students from the prejudices of their social milieu—of narrow-minded parents, for example, or guardians of 'morality'. But to ask him to have a policy also for the philistines, to have a scheme into which they can fit—that is entirely idle. They will be busy whatever he does; and he has enough to do combating them. Incidental to this combat, certainly, will be the making of compromises, of a certain composition of claims, in the institutions in which both sides are working; but the liberal will have no 'loyalty' to any such adjustment, he will continually seek a more favourable balance—recognizing, of course, that it is not always by frontal attacks that gains are made. And this, I contend, is a much more responsible attitude than any profession of caring for the interests of all, which means, in practice, a ruling out of liberality. Culture, it cannot be too strongly urged, is a special interest and requires, for its persistence, a certain irreconcilability.[8]

For Anderson, then, the field of education itself, as well as any particular educational institution, is

a battlefield between liberality and illiberality—between cosmopolitanism and patriotism, between the treatment of the child as 'the heir of all the ages' and the treatment of him as job-fodder. And practical-

[8] 'Education and Practicality', see pp. 157–8.

ity, for the liberal, consists in keeping up this opposition, with the realization that while he can never get control of the system, he also can never be ousted from it. For any sort of education must involve a certain amount of freethinking; it must treat of certain *subjects*, and these cannot be completely canalized or directed to external ends —they must, to some extent, be developed in their own terms. Thus, while the contemporary attack on subjects and concern with the 'ends' of education are symptoms of educational decline, there are countervailing tendencies; and the person who thinks he can harness education to 'welfare' is unpractical, as well as untheoretical, in his misunderstanding of his material. A training dominated by the conception of utility, by the treatment of certain conditions of life as peculiarly *ends*, is a training in gullibility; but, in having any sort of subject-matter, it cannot entirely exclude criticism, even if it falls short in the *exposition* of critical method and the exposure of pre-judice.[9]

The conflict between what Anderson calls the 'liberal' and the 'illiberal' view of education, involves, in modern conditions, the conflict between classicism and utilitarianism as two opposing views of culture—a conflict he brought out in his lectures on education and in his 'Address on Classicism' by counterposing the views of Matthew Arnold in *Culture and Anarchy*, *Essays in Criticism* and *Literature and Dogma* with those of Robert Owen's *A New View of Society* and Herbert Spencer's *Essays on Education*,[10] with their philistine and con-fused elevation of the need for bare survival and procreation over the survival of kinds and ways of life and their relegation of culture and art to activities for leisure. In spite of his own initial education in the sciences, and in opposition to the dominant trend in Scottish university education and educational discussions in his own day, Anderson took the view that

[9] Ibid., pp. 156–7.
[10] Matthew Arnold, *Culture and Anarchy*, London, 1869; Matthew Arnold, *Essays in Criticism*, London, 1863; Matthew Arnold, *Literature and Dogma*, London, 1873; Robert Owen, *A New View of Society*, London 1813; Herbert Spencer, *Essays on Education*, Everyman, London 1911.

the promotion of science as the central educational subject or set of subjects was linked with utilitarianism and the elevation of *practical* over *intellectual* ends. Ths main argument is worth repeating here, in his own words:

To claim educational pre-eminence for the classics, or simply to present classicism as an important view of culture, would commonly in these times be met with ridicule or indifference, since neither the notion of culture nor the classical outlook is now accorded any great respect even in reputedly educated circles. At the outset of the intense struggles, which have occupied the past century or more, over the nature and organization of education, the conception of it as 'liberal' and hence classical was widespread and apparently well-entrenched. But the position has changed so radically that nowadays it is rare to find any greater concession made to liberal study, either in the narrower sense of concentration on the 'classical tongues' or in the broader sense of attention to the major productions of humane letters, than that it is a harmless eccentricity which may still for a time occupy its small corner. What is of special educational importance, it is widely maintained, is study of the sciences; for, while liberal study had at no time an intrinsically greater capacity for developing the mind, it has under present conditions a very much slighter power of bringing us to a serious grappling with our vital problems. And this is in line with the view which prevails among professional education-ists who even though the main emphasis is not always on science, conceive education as the preparation of the pupil for the problems of the real world in which he is to live, and on that principle dismiss the upholder of tradition as a follower of phantasies.

It is open to the traditionalists to reply that preparation for grap-pling with what is contemporary does not necessarily involve con-centration on the *study* of what is contemporary and that the setting aside of tradition, of 'the best that has been thought and said' on major human problems, may well be the way to miss their solution. But first it may be pointed out that the classical and the utilitarian views of education are distinguished as employing intrinsic and extrinsic criteria, the one considering education in its own character, as the development of thinking or criticism, the other considering it in its contribution to something else, subordinating it in this way to the non-educational and running the greatest risk of distorting its character. For clearly there can be no subject or field of study which is utilitarian in itself, whose character resides in what it produces or helps to produce, and this applies as much to science as to any other study; its intrinsic character, taken as the search for laws, the study of the ways of working of actual things, has no reference to the turning of its findings to 'practical' account. But there can be no doubt that science as currently understood is concerned with the production of results, with the making of physical translations and transformations, and that, in the view of many scientific practitioners, science even enjoins us to produce this result rather than that.

In so far as science is regarded in this way, it is assimilated to the theology which at one time it seemed destined to displace; it also is supplementing consideration of what is the case by injunctions to us to seek the means by which we may be saved. A topical example of such salvationist thinking is to be found in agitations for peace, in which, leaving aside any attempt to determine the objective conditions either of the occurrence of international conflicts themselves or of the discovery of the truth concerning them, it is assumed that anything that is 'undesirable' can, by a sufficiency of protests or 'appeals to reason', be eliminated. . . .

The connection between the trend to a more and more 'scientific' education and the conception of education as having to be directed beyond itself to social usefulness, to 'serving the community' in non-educational ways, falls within the same chapter of ideas. Such external direction, however weak its theoretical foundation, is an inescapable contemporary phenomenon, and it is responsible not only for the steady fall in educational standards, the slighter and slighter *literacy* of the supposedly educated, but for what may fairly be called the growing industrialization of educational institutions. This is exhibited not merely in their directing students to industry and thus engaging in the provision of the techniques which industry requires, but in their becoming themselves more and more technological, applying techniques of teaching, overcoming 'wastage', learning how to turn out the maximum number of technicians—and losing scholarship in the process. This external view of the function of *universities* in particular is one of the leading notes of the Murray report, however it may be blended with pious phrases in the older mode. Thus, to the Committee's contention that 'the universities are or should be the guardians of intellectual standards and intellectual integrity in the community',[11] it can be retorted that they cannot be such guardians if their work is subordinated to *other* standards, if they are serving a postulated unity of interests ('the community') of which the intellectual interest is only a part. Nothing short of a rejection of this imaginary 'common good' (something that satisfies every interest and every person) can maintain at their proper intellectual level institutions whose work is criticism or the examination of all assumptions. The carrying out of this work requires them to recognize that they are one of a number of *competing* social forces and that what, for example, is industry's gain is quite commonly education's loss.

The conception of education as an industry, then, with its raw materials, machines, machine-minders and turned-out goods, is opposed to the conception of it as conversion, a turning round of the mind, or, as Arnold has it in his definition of culture (*Culture and Anarchy*, Preface), the turning of 'a stream of fresh and free thought upon our stock notions and habits'.[12]

Understandably, Anderson had no high view of the educational 'theories' and 'philosophies' of education that passed for important or significant, that attracted public attention and acclaim, in his day. He would have been no more impressed—if anything, less impressed—with those that do so today. Criticism of the instrument as a substitute for doing the work was to him always a poor and misguided activity; he saw no evidence that the theorists of education had educated or educational theories. He attacked the pretensions of educational theorists—their voluntaristic belief that theirs was a rational mind standing outside society and capable of remoulding its members anew, and he attacked their constant subordination of education to something else—to religious, patriotic and solidarist dogmas, ideologies and illusions, to

[11] *Report of the Committee on Australian Universities*, 1957, p. 120, 'Summary and Conclusions'.
[12] 'Classicism', pp. 43–6.

practical ends and utilities, to the service of industry or society, to the abstract individual and the confused conception of self-development. The long and enthusiastic struggle by Anderson and his disciples against religion in education, against censorship, indoctrination and training were all a direct outcome of these views—a defence of culture and its requirements against dogmatism, suppression and the elevation of non- or anti-culture and non- or anti-educational requirements. His belief in academic freedom was simply a belief in free thought and unrestricted criticism, coupled with the belief that such a spirit of inquiry was a particular social interest lodged in particular social institutions that acted as its custodians. Of these the university was the most important and any attempts to subordinate its central concern with criticism and inquiry was to be resisted at all costs. In his own day, and to a significant extent in ours, such threats came from the state, from religious and patriotic 'authorities', from demands that the university serve the 'community' and uphold what is alleged to be 'its' ideology. Within educational institutions, increasingly since the Second World War, such threats came as much as, if not more than, from the Left as the Right, from students as from 'authorities', but Anderson always recognized that the university, like any other institution, was not a cohesive single-minded community—that the struggle for the academic had to be waged within it, against other trends in the institution, just as it had to be waged outside it against other trends in society. The academic constituted what was distinctive about the university, what gave it a coherent tradition and policy, but it neither pervaded the whole of the university nor stopped within its walls.

'A university,' I wrote some years ago,

is neither a microcosm of society nor a Temple of Youth. A university as an institution is concerned with and embodies a *particular* social interest—the interest in truth as a condition of culture, of rationality and rational action, of technical competence and social and intellectual judgement. A university as an institution is thus concerned with promoting the *discipline* of inquiry, the *intellectual organization* of knowledge, the *rigour* of argument and the *drawing of distinctions* between the true and the false, the good and the bad, the relevant and the irrelevant, the competent and the incompetent. There are good universities and bad universities, good professors and bad professors, good students and bad students. It is not the role of a university to make everyone, the good and the bad alike, feel equally at home and important within the university. A university is anti-authoritarian in the sense that it accepts no authority but the authority of rational argument; it demands, in principle, that intellectual competence and intellectual status be proved, over and over again, by actual performance in argument and intellectual endeavour. But a university has no time for that crude Communism which Karl Marx denounced—the Communism which wants to eliminate all distinctions of quality and character, which wishes to abolish talent by force. This is the sentimental romanticism of nihilism, the 'abstract negation'—as Karl Marx called it—'of the whole world of culture and civilization', which is in fact a camouflaged form of universal envy, seeking to destroy what it cannot appropriate.

My remarks were directed toward attitudes and dangers not as prevalent, in this particular form, in Anderson's day, but I believe he would have found the assertions familiar and agreed with them. Further, he stressed to an extent rarely heard today, the gulf between universities and technical colleges, between students and 'trainees', and bitterly opposed any breach of the sharp distinction he drew between an institution whose central function is the promotion of criticism and inquiry and institutions whose central function is something else. This was not for him, as it has become for so many polytechnic teachers and students, a matter of 'class' division: the 'Barbarians' pursuing their rowing blues are no more caught up in critical inquiry than the 'Philistines' seeking their technical qualifications to increase their salaries and advance their status.

The answer to the question 'How would you run a school or

university?' then, for Anderson as for me, is 'with intelligent, cultured, educated teachers, who see their task as the interest in and promotion of culture, of inquiry, of critical understanding, of knowledge no matter where it leads, who teach us to frame hypotheses and test them, to revise our opinions in the light of the results, to want to know *why*, to reject all authority but that of logical argument and empirical observation.' The school, or the university, as an actual institution, in a given time and place, will have many other demands made on it—to 'teach' children road safety, hygiene, drug avoidance, love of their neighbours, social accomplishments and useful skills, patriotism or respect for the 'human qualities' of the uneducated and 'deprived', charity, sympathy and obedience. In so far as these demands do not involve or amount to the elevation of falsehoods or confusions, or to deliberate attempts at indoctrination, at stifling critical responses or avoiding critical thought, they will, for their fulfilment, be parasitic on education, on the development of knowledge and understanding, on the capacity to think critically. But in so far as they elevate goals other than the development of knowledge and understanding, they will be extra- or anti-educational, distracting attention from the educational work of the school, competing with it and, all too often, distorting it. The teacher or director, as a person operating in a concrete social context, competing for material support, resources, etcetera, will be critical of such trends but often unable to resist them totally, forced into accommodations, into spending his time on non-educational matters, or subsidiary and ancillary ones. But if so, he will insist on differentiating the activities involved, separating education from various forms of training and opposing, at each step, further encroachments by the latter upon the educational field—resisting the constant attempt, by those serving other interests, to blur the distinction. As an educated person, as one whose exercise of critical intelligence and study of culture and cultures has led him, as I believe it must, to the recognition of pluralism, of the existence of competing interests and ways of life and to the rejection of the claims of the spokesmen of solidarism and imposed authority to be above these conflicts, he will be a political democrat; he will recognize, I believe, the existence of other interests and other claims than those of education, and, as a person whose concerns are not confined to education, respond to them. But he will be quick to see, and jealous to guard against, the destructive edge that such interests and claims can and do turn against the educational interest—the educational disaster, for example, that can and does result from a levelling conception of 'schooling for democracy' that suppresses or ignores the distinction between educational capacities, involvement and application, and brings education, language and thinking down to the level and interest of all, that is, down to the level of the lowest common denominator.

A great deal of the more 'practical', allegedly 'concrete' side of the contemporary philosophy of education and educational theory, apart from being based on slanted and conceptually confused notions of ethics, 'personality', 'education' and 'research', is based on a bureaucratic presupposition that teachers are and will be unintelligent, that they must be given 'guidance' and 'theory' to direct them in matters that in fact require intelligent and flexible response. The assumption may be justified; if it is, the 'theory' will do little to rectify the situation. Neither 'teaching techniques' nor 'learning techniques' are a substitute for thinking. This is as true in so-called 'curriculum construction' as in 'methods of assessment', in the selection of particular areas of study as in the decision on how to approach and present them. Bureaucratization is strengthened, not weakened, by the extension of an abstract doctrine of (political) 'rights' to the school and the university. The unintelligence of the educational 'authorities' themselves comes out in their constant tendency to violent swings from one extreme to another—from rigid streaming to undifferentiated schooling, from disciplines to projects, from 'old' mathematics to 'new' mathematics, from distinct scientific disciplines to unified science, and then back again, and in their more recent obsession with manufacturing the evidence for educational equality by manipulating the results. What is lacking in all this, in the attempt to serve all interests at once, is a rudder—a conception of the intrinsic nature and requirements of education, in terms of which new methods and proposals can be assessed and cautiously experimented with. And the more 'scientific' or 'democratic' educational theory and educational theorists become, the *less* grasp they have of culture or education itself.

The philosophy and the practice of education, then, require what Anderson sought to give them—a conception of culture, of criticism, of the nature of progress in knowledge and capacity for argument, rather than a set of techniques for 'communication' or a social philosophy for all from which educational practices are to be deduced. The concern with culture, with knowledge and the development of critical understanding, will require us, as Anderson argued, to recognize distinct subjects, fields of inquiry, with their own special laws, but not with their own special truth. We will see in education, and in the interrelation of these fields, the unity of culture and the common logic of inquiry, of the analysis of problems and the conduct of argument and experiment. For Anderson, linguistic and literary studies stand at the centre, at least of the earlier phases of education as the introduction to culture—linguistic studies in their conveying of connections and distinctions in the world, their concern with precision and with language as a repository of culture; literature as the concrete study of the human and the social, an area in which political and ethical insights are often more highly developed and certainly more accessible to the child than in abstract social and ethical theory, though all study is finally philosophical. But to emphasize this, of course, is also to emphasize that the child studies important literary productions, not that it reads works allegedly accessible to it or interesting for it because they make no demands on imagination or thought, but appeal to fantasy and the child's love of itself and its own image. The achievements of science (for example Darwin's conception of evolution) were for Anderson a necessary part of historical and philosophical understanding. It was the manipulative character of scientific training, its emphasis on practicality, that made Anderson reluctant to see it as a centrally educational subject. The critical capacities of scientists as a class—as opposed, for example, to their musical abilities—do much to suggest he was right; so do the attitudes and confusions now involved in the elevation of biology and environmental studies as central, allegedly 'guiding' studies, enabling us to see our 'real' nature and our 'place in the world'.

The educational interest, the concern with culture and criticism, now as always, has to fight for its existence on many fronts, against powerful, indeed dominant, illusions and anti-educational interests. The fashion in illusions, the language of salvationism and obscurantism, changes with remarkable rapidity, attacks come from new and sometimes unexpected quarters—though much that we see today is the culmination of more general social trends which Anderson was attacking in the 1940s. There is much more to be said, in detail, about the philosophy of education than Anderson said; the extension of it is so difficult, and the general performance in it is so poor, because educational theory as the theory of culture and as 'applied theory', as the study of learning and its relation to character, organization, etcetera involves, in a subsidiary way, many of the most subtle problems of philosophy, calling for tough-minded resistance to the fashionable, while its practitioners, having no single intellectual discipline of their own, readily fall for the fashionable and the superficial in their confused and vicious attempt to satisfy all interests and serve all masters at once, to evolve a 'total' theory of society, schooling and the child. Against this, I believe, Anderson said the important and central things without which we can have no philosophy of education, or as I would prefer to put it, no *conception* of either education or culture as central and complex human traditions, not tools for the *attainment* of other ends. That there is still far more to be said about the role of non-intellectual factors in learning, about the complex intertwining of motives, social forces and traditions, is not a reason for abandoning the clarity and intransigence about what is central which he consistently called for.

Part II

ESSAYS ON EDUCATION

4

Classicism

To claim educational pre-eminence for the classics, or simply to present classicism as an important view of culture, would commonly in these times be met with ridicule or indifference, since neither the notion of culture nor the classical outlook is now accorded any great respect even in reputedly educated circles. At the outset of the intense struggles, which have occupied the past century or more, over the nature and organization of education, the conception of it as 'liberal' and hence classical was widespread and apparently well-entrenched. But the position has changed so radically that nowadays it is rare to find any greater concession made to liberal study, either in the narrower sense of concentration on the 'classical tongues' or in the broader sense of attention to the major productions of humane letters, than that it is a harmless eccentricity which may still for a time occupy its small corner. What is of special educational importance, it is widely maintained, is study of the sciences; for, while liberal study had at no time an intrinsically greater capacity for developing the mind, it has under present conditions a very much slighter power of bringing us to a serious grappling with our vital problems. And this is in line with the view which prevails among professional educationists who, even though the main emphasis is not always on science, conceive education as the preparation of the pupil for the problems of the real world in which he is to live, and on that principle dismiss the upholder of tradition as a follower of fantasies.

It is open to the traditionalists to reply that preparation for grappling with what is contemporary does not necessarily involve concentration on the *study* of what is contemporary and that the setting aside of tradition, of 'the best that has been thought and said' on major human problems, may well be the way to miss their solution. But first it may be pointed out that the classical and the utilitarian views of education are distinguished as employing intrinsic and extrinsic criteria, the one considering education in its own character, as the development of thinking or criticism, the other considering it in its contribution to something else, subordinating it in this way to the non-educational and running the greatest risk of distorting its character. For clearly there can be no subject or field of study which is utilitarian in itself, whose character resides in what it produces or helps to produce, and this applies as much to science as to any other study; its intrinsic character, taken as the search for laws, the study of the ways of working of actual things, has no reference to the turning of its findings to 'practical' account. But there can be no doubt that science as currently understood is concerned with the production of results, with the making of physical translations and transformations, and that, in the view of many scientific practitioners, science even enjoins us to produce this result rather than that.

In so far as science is regarded in this way, it is assimilated to the theology which at one time it seemed destined to displace; it also is supplementing consideration of what is the case by injunctions to us to seek the means by which we may be saved. A topical example of such salvationist thinking is to be found in agitations for peace, in which, leaving aside any attempt to determine the objective conditions either of the occurrence of international conflicts themselves or of the discovery of the truth concerning them, it is assumed that anything that is 'undesirable' can, by a sufficiency of protests or 'appeals to reason', be eliminated. The implication is that there are no natural laws in the social or political sphere—for, if there were, there would be certain things which, under given conditions,

could not be eliminated, since they were necessary consequences of those conditions. But it is no way scientific to
suppose that there is any field of occurrences not marked by
regularities, and it is scarcely less naive to represent the social
field as one in which there are a few simple truths which can be
grasped without intensive study and which are already sufficiently recognized. The maintaining of such views holds out
no prospect of assistance to the settlement of matters of practical urgency; it operates merely as an obstacle to *inquiry* into
social affairs in general and international affairs in particular. It
is still important to note that the belief, increasingly popular
since the days of Spencer and Huxley, that science can prescribe practical policies, rests on the assumption that society
itself is not a subject of science. But this in turn carries the
implication that science has nothing to contribute to society's
development.

The connection between the trend to a more and more
'scientific' education and the conception of education as having to be directed beyond itself to social usefulness, to 'serving
the community' in non-educational ways, falls within the
same chapter of ideas. Such external direction, however weak
its theoretical foundation, is an inescapable contemporary
phenomenon, and it is responsible not only for the steady fall
in educational standards, the slighter and slighter *literacy* of the
supposedly educated, but for what may fairly be called the
growing industrialization of educational institutions. This is
exhibited not merely in their directing students to industry
and thus engaging in the provision of the techniques which
industry requires, but in their becoming themselves more and
more technological, applying techniques of teaching, overcoming 'wastage', learning how to turn out the maximum
number of technicians—and losing scholarship in the process.
This external view of the function of *universities* in particular is
one of the leading notes of the Murray report, however it may
be blended with pious phrases in the older mode. Thus, to the
Committee's contention that 'the universities are or should be

the guardians of intellectual standards and intellectual integrity in the community',[1] it can be retorted that they cannot be such guardians if their work is subordinated to *other* standards, if they are serving a postulated unity of interests ('the community') of which the intellectual interest is only a part. Nothing short of a rejection of this imaginary 'common good' (something that satisfies every interest and every person) can maintain at their proper intellectual level institutions whose work is criticism or the examination of all assumptions. The carrying out of this work requires them to recognize that they are one of a number of *competing* social forces and that what, for example, is industry's gain is quite commonly education's loss.

The conception of education as an industry, then, with its raw materials, machines, machine-minders and turned-out goods, is opposed to the conception of it as conversion, a turning round of the mind, or, as Arnold has it in his definition of culture (*Culture and Anarchy*, Preface), the turning of 'a stream of fresh and free thought upon our stock notions and habits'. It is true that Arnold himself is still somewhat bemused by the stock notion of 'the common good', but, at least, in 'The Function of Criticism at the present time' (*Essays in Criticism*, First Series, I) he allows that the 'mass of mankind will never have any ardent zeal for seeing things as they are', and that men will be content for the most part to rest their practice on very inadequate ideas. 'For', as he puts it even more forcibly on an earlier page, 'what is at present the bane of criticism in this country? It is that practical considerations cling to it and stifle it. It subserves interests not its own. Our organs of criticism are organs of men and parties having practical ends to serve, and with them those practical ends are the first thing and the play of mind the second; so much play of mind as is compatible with the prosecution of those practical ends is all that is wanted.'

[1] *Report of the Committee on Australian Universities*, 1957, p. 120, 'Summary and Conclusions'.

Concentration on what serves one's purposes, satisfaction with the 'just as good' or the 'good enough to get there', exists even more strikingly and influentially in public life at present than it did in Arnold's time, and it has penetrated more and more deeply into education, promoting shoddy thinking and slipshod language in the name of social equality and amelioration and other 'inadequate ideas' which have less and less critical intelligence applied to them. It is not surprising, in particular, that pupils should be turned out with a poor sense of the English language, when their teachers are concerned to propagate and benefit by the whole range of meliorist and utilitarian ideas and, in their satisfaction with what 'gets across' in this way, feel no impulse towards the largeness of view and precision of thought which would require its remoulding and which would stimulate sensitive expression. The 'practical end' of taking one's place in the community, of securing more or less useful and remunerative occupation, overshadows critical thinking; and, to draw more fully on Arnold's terminology, the function of education at the present time is substantially that of turning the populace into Philistines.

Incidentally, Arnold's notion of 'practical ends' is a somewhat loose and uncritical one. To take anything as an end is presumably to regard it as capable of actually coming about—of coming about, as we say, 'in practice'. It is not apparent, on this basis, how practical ends could be distinguished from any other ends. A distinction might be attempted in terms of the common antithesis of practice and theory, and practical outcomes of human activity might then be taken as those which were not theoretical—not, that is to say, as states which could not be *objects* of thought but as states which had no *thinking* embodied in them. Much of what is actually produced by contemporary education may well be of this unthinking character, but where thinking, as contrasted with conformity and intellectual vacuity, does emerge from the process, it can hardly be dismissed as unpractical—it may have distinctly more social force than much that passes as practical. Arnold would have been speaking more to the purpose if, instead of distinguishing types of ends, he had distinguished between concentration on ends, on definite objects to be secured, and the carrying on of certain activities (in particular, the activity of inquiry) without regard to any such programme; but this is a conception at which he does not arrive.

In fact, while Arnold's contribution to the understanding of these questions is considerable, he makes in a number of places undue concessions to practice and fails in critical elucidation of its character. This is notably so in his discussion of 'Hellenism and Hebraism' (*Culture and Anarchy*, Ch. IV) when he contrasts the uppermost Hellenic idea, 'to see things as they really are', with the uppermost Hebraic idea of 'conduct and obedience', or, in his alternative formulation, 'spontaneity of consciousness' with 'strictness of conscience', and treats the two not as antagonistic but as complementary sides of culture. Apart from the fairly obvious objection that conscience has an adverse effect on the free play of intellect (if, indeed, it does not *spring* from intellectual narrowness), Arnold does not explain why conduct is not just one of the things to be seen as they are, or how it can be regarded as raising any distinct *type* of problem. Certainly, in *Literature and Dogma* (Ch. I), he distinguishes speculative problems concerning human character or activity from 'practical' problems, the merely theoretical difficulty of finding what happens from the difficulty of *doing* 'what we very well know ought to be done', that is, in his view, the 'difficulty of religion' which 'extends to rightness in the whole range of what we call *conduct*; in three-fourths, therefore, at the very lowest computation, of human life.' But he definitely does not mean that such problems are solved *ambulando*, that it just so happens that we sometimes do what 'ought' to be done, whatever we might know or think about it; the question is always of the solution of a speculative problem, of finding out that something *is the case*—for example, that doing what is right is contingent on the acceptance of a certain kind of guidance—though it might still be argued, in this connection that 'right' and 'ought' are stock notions we should have to dispense with if our speculation on conduct went any distance. Perhaps it is some sense of the weakness of his doctrine of conduct that leads Arnold into the bathos of his concluding observation in the section of his argument to which I am referring: 'And so, when we are asked, what is the object of religion?—let us reply: *Conduct*. And when we are asked further, what is conduct?—let us answer: *Three-fourths of life.*'

But however strongly all this may point to the conclusion that no account can be given of culture as a conjunction of Hellenism and Hebraism, this would be nothing against the account of it as Hellenism itself, that is, 'seeing things as they are'—adopting the objective as against the subjective out-look—turning critical intelligence on all subjects, including (and perhaps especially) the subject of human activities. Such an account, of course, would not imply that Greek civilization, even in its 'classical' period (the period of the flourishing of objectivism, criticism, intellectual detachment), was objectiv-ist through and through. It is, indeed, part of the classicist position to see that this cannot be the case, to see, as in the notable example of Socrates,[2] that culture exists in the struggle with superstition and backwardness. Socrates upheld the objective treatment of all subjects—and specifically of the subjects, such as religion, ethics, aesthetics, in which subjectiv-ism still seeks a refuge; he combated subjectivism alike in the form of Sophistic conventionalism ('Man is the measure of all things') and in that of Athenian democratism ('The people are the measure of all things'). Remarkably enough, it is largely

---

[2] On the Socratic philosophy I very largely follow the views of John Burnet, whose work on Socrates and on Greek philosophy generally, neg-lected though it is in these days, seems to me to make a remarkable contribu-tion both to classicism and to philosophy, and whose wholeness of view provides a striking contrast to the piecemeal 'philosophies' which are now in vogue.

from the force of his criticisms that his opponents retain a place in the history of civilization. And what these criticisms bring out is the difference between the reality and the pretence of knowledge, whether the pretenders were reputedly learned men or, like his prosecutors, men who thought that knowledge—of morals in particular—came from immersion in civic life and did not require or admit of formal scrutiny and the raising of difficulties. Here for the first time in the history of thought we encounter the notion of 'practical truth', of knowledge without study, of assertions that cannot be challenged because they are backed by the process of living. The position is illustrated again in the case of the contemporary evangelical who, in saying 'He's real to me', imagines that he has provided a sanction for certain lines of action, though engaging in them has no demonstrable connection with the postulated sanctioning figure. It is this 'practical' jumping over of problems that Socrates was specially concerned to expose. And, as he predicted, even the practical expedient of slaying him furnished no escape from the difficulties he had raised.

But neither the position nor the influence of Socrates can be described as exclusively objectivist. That there is in his doctrines a streak of romanticism or mysticism (even though this can often be treated as merely a trimming round a realist or empiricist core) is clear enough from his belief in 'ultimates', entities standing above the actual movement of things. This is in striking contrast with the thorough-going objectivism of his predecessor, Heraclitus, who was unremitting in his attack on subjectivist illusions, on the operation of desire or the imagining of things as we should like them to be, as opposed to the operation of understanding or the finding of things (including our own activities) as they positively are, with no granting of a privileged position in reality to gods, men or molecules, with conflict everywhere and nothing above the battle. His criticism was directed especially against the school of Pythagoreans (whence much of it could in turn have been directed against Socrates)—against their little absolutes or atomic realities; against their distortion of their material from a desire for simplicity, for the tidy and complete solution; against the division of the unhistorical from the historical, of the exact from the inexact. This last point recalls Arnold's distinction (again in Ch. I of *Literature and Dogma*) between 'a term of science or exact knowledge' and 'a term of poetry and eloquence'—and here the Heraclitean or objectivist position is that no line can be drawn between these, that there can be no defensible claim to knowledge of distinct things which have no common measures, which do not exist in the same situations and enter into joint transactions. And, in particular, there is the implication that we can no more have quantity without quality than we can have quality without quantity or otherwise than as spatio-temporal process.

But while Heraclitus had this sense of the interlocking of all materials and all problems, he had by no means worked out a critical apparatus (a doctrine of types of problem and forms of solution in any inquiry) in the way that Socrates, followed by Plato, did. And thus for a general conception of the objectivist outlook, of classicism on its basic *philosophical* side, of the 'judgement' which applies to all subjects and the 'literalism' which is always ruinous to inquiry, we have to go to both these sources; they together set up the model of philosophical Hellenism, and, even though the other contributors to the thought of the period did not reach the same level, these would suffice to make it a classical period—a period in which disinterestedness stands out from the wrangle of special interests as it does not do in culturally lower times.

It is in so far as it has followed the Greek model that modern philosophy has also had a classical character, though it has had to fight against an even more debilitating modernism (or 'up-to-dateness') than that of the Sophists. This modernism comes out strikingly in the work of the two thinkers who have been commonly regarded as the founders of modern philosophy—Bacon and Descartes. We need not perhaps take very seriously Descartes' reported remarks that he was proud of

having forgotten the Greek which he had learned as a boy, and
that Latin, lauded as 'the language of Cicero', was just as much
the language of Cicero's serving-maid—though it might be
observed in passing that an infusion of the Hellenic spirit may
persist beyond the recalling of Greek words, and that it is not
true that 'the same language' is used by the learned and the
vulgar, that, on the contrary, it is pre-eminently in *letters* that a
language has its characteristic existence.[3] What is more to the
purpose in both thinkers is their practicalism and progressivism, illustrated in Bacon's view that the 'end of the sciences is
their usefulness to the human race' and that to 'increase knowledge is to extend the dominion of man over nature, and so to
increase his comfort and happiness, so far as these depend on
external circumstances',[4] and in the view of Descartes that the
intellectual advance consequent on his own discoveries 'would
have far-reaching effects on the condition of mankind' and in
his first proposed title for the *Discourse on Method*, 'The Project
of a Universal Science which can elevate our Nature to its
highest degree of Perfection.'[5]

Adamson[6] says that to both Bacon and Descartes 'the
scholastic logic presented itself as the essence of a thoroughly
false and futile method of knowledge. . . . Both thinkers were
animated by the spirit of reformation in science, and both
emphasise the practical end of all speculation. For both, therefore, logic, which to neither is of high value, appeared to be a
species of practical science, a generalized statement of the
mode in which intellect acquires new knowledge, in which the

---

[3] Many of the errors of our day are linked with the delusion that a 'spoken
language' means what is spoken by the unlearned mass (which, as Arnold
has indicated, is too much concerned with immediate 'practical' objects to
trouble about the finer distinctions and connections embodied in learned
speech and writing) and that resistance to the incorporation of vulgar
locutions in the recognized language is mere pedantry and archaism.

[4] J. B. Bury, *The Idea of Progress*, London, 1920, p. 58.

[5] Ibid., p. 67.

[6] Robert Adamson, *A Short History of Logic*, ed. W. R. Sorley, London
1911, p. 85.

mind proceeds from known to unknown.' This degradation of the subject, logic, to the status of an instrument or set of devices is typical of the practicalist or instrumentalist outlook (though it still cannot show how deviser and devised can enter into common situations or, as the phrase goes, 'exist in the same world'), and it may be compared to recent views of scientific method (which is actually logic, considered in terms of types of questions that can arise in inquiry) as simply the procedures of scientists. The matter is illustrated again in the contempt of the two thinkers for syllogism (in fact, the commonest as well as the most fruitful form of demonstrative reasoning) and its replacement by the Baconian 'induction' and the Cartesian 'intuition'. But 'induction', where it is not syllogism disguised, is at best fallacious reasoning and at worst mere guesswork—though it is interestingly related to that great region of modern science (reminiscent of Pythagorean doctrine) in which ignorance is treated as a kind of knowledge, uncertainty as a kind of certainty. And 'intuition', again where it is not disguised syllogism, is merely knowledge divorced from any possibility of its being acquired by a mind, i.e., knowing without learning.

The anti-classicism of Descartes comes out not merely in his antipathy to history and tradition, but in his proposing, as the ground of the distinction of men from animals, an abstract rationality in place of the concrete and many-sided culture (language and literature, law, investigation, etcetera) which really does distinguish them. This lack of concreteness is characteristic of the whole modernist position; it is bound up with that opposition to quality or distinction which is a recurrent feature of modern thought (in the social as in other spheres), and one expression of which is proof by identities and not by concrete facts. It comes out in Descartes' epistemological approach to philosophy which proved so influential in later thought and which gives the question of our power of comprehending actualities priority to that of actualities themselves. This, however, can readily be seen to be a quite confused position; for knowledge of our cognitive powers does not set us on the way to detailed knowledge of the actual unless they also are actual, and, if they are, they have no higher standing as objects of cognition than other cognizable things. The difficulty is merely evaded by Descartes in his doctrine of self-knowledge (his *cogito ergo sum*), since, on the one hand, there is still no logical passage from self-knowledge to knowledge of other things, and, on the other hand, knowledge of a real self would have to be of its concrete characters and not of mere dispositions or capacities. The Cartesian *cogito*, then, is rooted in ambiguity; it derives such plausibility as it has from its assigning all the parts in a complex relationship to the same thing. But it does so at the cost of content; the certainty it can be taken to give us is not the certainty of any particular thing but, at most, the certainty of 'certainty itself'. Its certainty, in other words, is indistinguishable from its emptiness.

This criticism of the *cogito* is moderately familiar; what is not so commonly recognized is that criticism of the same sort applies to those other prominent features of modernist doctrine, its utilitarianism and its progressivism—that their plausibility also is grounded in their lack of content. Ordinarily, to call anything useful is to say that it brings about something else—more specifically, perhaps, brings about something wanted—but since there is no limit to the range of things that people want, since anything might be wanted by someone, the effective meaning of useful is just *having effects*, and this covers anything whatever. On this interpretation, it would be idle for a person to say that he supports 'utility', for he would not be supporting any distinguishable thing. But the utilitarian does not want to say that he supports the indefinite going on of things; he wants to affirm the existence of definite stopping-places; he wants to recognize, beyond the mere relation of producing or bringing about, 'absolute utilities'— things which have their usefulness in themselves or as part of their own character. And here again we have a quite empty conception—the conception of the attainment of 'attainment' or the satisfaction in 'satisfaction' and not in any concrete thing.

In the same way, 'progress' can only mean the going on of what goes on, or the futurity of the future, unless the question is of the progress not of 'things in general' but of a distinct class of things, things of some specific quality. And, even working with a rough-and-ready conception of the 'flourishing' of such a class, we can never find more than risings and fallings (the strengthening of such things at certain times and places, matched by their weakening at other times and places) and thus can find no reason for belief in a law of their progress, let alone a law of universal progress. Such beliefs rest on belief in a 'scheme of things', but a scheme which is always fragmentarily conceived and gives no ground on which it may be demonstrated that one form of activity rather than another is bound to thrive. And an even more serious defect of progressivist doctrines is that they are doctrines of betterment, that is, of higher and lower *degrees* of goodness; and this, if goodness is a quality, is unintelligible, and, if it is not, is a measurement of things on an unknown scale and brings us back to the verbiage of 'evolutionary ethics', according to which the later is, of its very nature, the better—in other words, to the peddling of identities in the guise of information. It may be added that doctrines like utilitarianism and progressivism whose special concern is the future are not merely anti-classical but are opposed to study, since the past is a field of study which can be constantly opened up, while the future is a field of conjecture or fantasy. It is in this way that pessimism or the sense of a steady cultural decline has greater affinity to learning than the optimistic belief in continual advance; it points to concrete models and to the great difficulty of maintaining standards, as against the facile belief that they will automatically rise. All these considerations bring out the emptiness of the modernist outlook, as contrasted with the fullness of the historical and classical.

The Cartesian doctrine of 'matter' is likewise lacking in

content; the doctrine that extension is the essence of the
material affirms the sameness of all things and eliminates all
quality and distinction (carrying egalitarianism right through
the universe!); it is a doctrine that could be founded only on a
fallacious working with identities, and yet it is still treated by
most scientists not as absurd but as commonplace, the real
distinguishing-marks of things being set aside as 'secondary'
or illusory. It is needless to dwell on the writhings of the
intellect by which Descartes tries to straddle the gulf between
mind and matter, and bring pure thought and pure extension
into relation; it is enough to say that, while only historical
actualities (alike material and moving) can be so related, it is
the empty abstractions which have penetrated modern
thought. Nevertheless, this penetration has emphasized the
fundamental weaknesses of the Cartesian antithesis of thought
and extension, active and passive, user and used—for it
emerges in the writings of the eighteenth century, above all in
the work of La Mettrie, that anything we concretely call *man* is
as much subject to external influences (as capable of being *used*)
as anything we call *matter*, and so would go over into the
passive side of reality if there were such a side; yet this is
combined, among these 'old materialists', with belief in a class
of men who are *users*, a section of society, as Marx puts it, set
above society in general, and concerned (however inexplic-
ably and however, on the original premises, hopelessly) to
raise the social level.

   This theoretical instability comes out in a specially grotesque way in Owen's *A New View of Society*, where, for
example, in the Third Essay, he passes directly from the doctrine of external determination ('the character of man is, without a single exception, always formed for him. . . . Man,
therefore, never did, nor is it possible that he ever can, form his
own character') to a call to action, to the question whether the
'substantial advantages' of the application of rational principles *should* be longer withheld from the mass of mankind and
the assertion that it is 'by the full and complete disclosure of

these principles that the destruction of ignorance and misery is to be effected, and the reign of reason, intelligence, and happiness is to be firmly established'. It is against such confusions, and with particular regard to how they affect education, that Marx directs the third of his Theses on Feuerbach, arguing that it is impossible to divide society into active and passive sections (whether conceived, implausibly enough, as *helpers* and *helped* or in any other manner), that there is no-one who is merely a victim of circumstances and no-one who is completely a master of circumstances, that there is interaction at all points. Or at least this last is the natural conclusion of the Thesis, but it is somewhat obscured and confused through Marx's obsession with the revolutionary re-making of society and the conflictless Utopia which he expects to see emerging.

Leaving aside, however, Marx's own inconsistencies and admitting the full force of his attack on Owen, we have still to recognize that it is meliorist ideas of the Owenite type that now prevail in public life and especially in the educational field. It is education above all that is overwhelmed by the flood of devotees of 'the fresh start', by those eloquent advocates of reform, satirized by Arnold (once more in 'The Function of Criticism'[7]), who are prepared to remodel all institutions on 'first principles', to the accompaniment of declamations like: 'Away with the notion of proceeding by any other course than the course dear to the Philistines; let us have a social movement, let us organize and combine a party to pursue truth and new thought, let us call it *the liberal party*, and let us all stick to each other and back each other up. Let us have no nonsense about independent criticism, and intellectual delicacy, and the few and the many. Don't let us trouble ourselves about foreign thought; we shall invent the whole thing for ourselves as we go along.' This, even though the names have changed,[8] is true

[7] Arnold, *Essays in Criticism*, Ch. I.
[8] That is, if *labour party* were taken as more appropriate to the current situation than *liberal party*, but it might be asked whether they are not all reformers together, nowadays.

to the character of current meliorism—improvisation, vague 'principles' (like 'development of personality') instead of a knowledge of and immersion in traditions, the overcoming of an intellectual resistance by the sheer weight of ignorance.

But, of course, there is less resistance than there was; the custodians of learning, shaken by the movement of the times, have to a quite considerable extent succumbed to modernism—or, at the best, are no longer masters of the case against it. One reason for this decline in critical power is that it is no longer expected of those who embark on a higher course of humane studies that they will give some serious attention to philosophy; accordingly, they are free to fall into as flagrant errors as Owen's and not even to have heard of the standard arguments against voluntarism or against utilitarianism and the whole sickly apparatus of welfare. Men with so narrowly specialized a training (even if it is called humane) do not understand that, if social conditions depend on the voluntary decisions which are made from time to time, there can be nothing properly called social or historical *theory* but merely *annals*, records of the various decisions made by various persons at various times—a source from which little in the way of critical thinking can spring. In the same way, they are ill-prepared for recognition of the serious intellectual decline, the loss of a sense of quality or distinction, involved in the reduction of ethics to a consideration of questions of distribution, of balanced shares in a single 'welfare fund'—as opposed to questions of qualitatively different forms of activity or ways of life which, whatever adjustments they may on occasion come to, can never be brought to a common denominator and will always be involved in conflicts.

It will still be the case that classicism, where it survives, will not give way to the *fears* which have encroached more and more on the academic domain—fear of the prevailing ideas, fear of *criticizing* democracy and reform, fear of giving offence to the multitude; for, as Socrates says in the *Crito*, though 'the many can kill us', that is no reason for setting their opinions on a level with the opinions of the wise, for believing, though they have a certain power over life and death, that they have any power over truth. There is no question here of putting forward classicism as a remedy for the ills of the time, of formulating slogans like 'Clear your mind of the cant of welfare and betterment' or 'Take arms against the sea of reforms.' The classicist recognizes the natural opposition between disinterestedness and interestedness, between concern with the ways of working of things themselves and concern with what we can get out of them. He will certainly note the special weakness of the objective outlook at the present time; he may even decide that our modern intellectual age, dating from the Renaissance, is on the verge of collapse and that a new barbarism is imminent; he can hardly fail to note the resemblance between current conditions and the decline of classical Greece, with the replacement of the solid thinking of the preceding time by a woolly-minded cosmopolitanism and humanitarianism. Whatever his conclusion on this point, he will continue, as a classicist, to work 'against the stream', as culture in all ages has had to work or (using the Hegelian terminology) as 'objective mind' has constantly had to struggle with the entanglements of 'bourgeois society', that is, the economic system. He will indeed observe the more and more direct *attacks* on culture, the constant pressure, on the part of those who want to make society 'go in the way it should', towards making learned institutions follow the same path, however much learning may thus be sacrificed. But the observation of this and other trends of a subjectivist and superstitious kind will be made in the course of exposing them and thus, as far as can still be done, bringing out the contrasting character of objectivism, of 'seeing things as they are'.

One important point here is the interrelatedness of the various departments of culture, and particularly the interlocking of cultural *studies*. I have spoken mainly of philosophy not just because it is my own subject of study but because I regard it as having a central place in any cultural system. If any other subject is to have a general apparatus of criticism, it can have it only by drawing upon philosophy—that is, on major contributions to the theory of objective reality and of the types of question that can be raised concerning any objective reality or actual subject. Thus the historian has to concern himself with questions of sequence and causality, the literary critic has to go into questions of form or structure, these being in either case primarily matters of logic. Each of them has his special lines of criticism; but, when we examine these, we find that they lead us in the same direction. The historian has his scrutiny of documents and weighing of testimony, but here not only is he confronted immediately with simple logical questions of the soundness or unsoundness of the inferences they present, or of the coherence of their materials, but he has to take account of types of human error and illusion, of obstacles to discovery, which can be elucidated only by reference to logic, to types of actual situations. The student of literature has, in turn, to have such knowledge of illusions as will enable him to understand the struggles of a character in their toils; he has, in addition, to see how such illusions import themselves into literary criticism itself, emerging in 'interpretations' (commonly of a romanticist or expressionist kind) which stand in the way of an objective view of the work.

In fact, what is broadly called 'judgement' (embracing knowledge of the basic types of objective issue and of the major types of human error) is operative in *all* criticism, and this is why all investigators in the cultural field are engaging in philosophy, even though they may not realize it—and why, again, the fact that it can no longer be taken for granted that a scholar in any field has undertaken some formal philosophical study, is indicative of cultural decline. The type of criticism, of exposure of error, most characteristic of classical or objectivist philosophy is that expressed by Plato in the phrase 'removing hypotheses', where the sort of supposition most injurious to thought and requiring most urgently to be got rid of is that which sets up distinct realms of being or of truth. The earliest object of critical attack here (though curiously it flourishes to this day) was on the scientific side, in such suppositions as that mathematical truth is of a different kind from physical truth—which would have the absurd consequence that no mathematical observation could be made on physical things. But the absurdity is no less when it is asserted (as it quite commonly is) that the figures and scenes of literature are the 'stuff of fancy', belonging to a different realm from that of ordinary things—which would mean that no critical comment whatever could be made on them, that literary theory would be contentless. The doctrine of 'realms' or 'worlds' is itself a fantasy (as Heraclitus was the first to point out); and the supposed hard-headedness of believers in an 'external world' (as contrasted with an inner world of thought) is simply theoretical muddlement. And here special mention may be made of Hegel as a classical figure in the modern period, who, in spite of some contamination by modernist doctrines, stead-ily opposed the breaking up of reality into separate realms, for whom philosophy was intertwined not merely with the broad history of thought but with history in general, who greatly stimulated philosophical interest in the work of the Greeks and who gave a great impetus to the development of objective aesthetics, objective ethics and objective social theory—of an objective view of the whole of culture.

His influence was considerable in the period I have referred to, in which it could be assumed that any scholar had studied philosophy, but also that any philosopher had engaged in a range of 'humane' studies and would retain these interests throughout his philosophical work, so that his philosophy would be in some measure both historical and literary, and its being so would be essential to his full development of critical judgement.[9] No-one could then have passed off as philosophy

[9] Reference may again be made to the work of Burnet in Greek philo-sophy, with its striking combination of philosophical and historical insight—bringing home to us the way in which knowledge of philosophy can help us to determine the course of philosophical thought and the views

the technical exercises which now pre-empt the field, and which mark the latest stage in the twentieth century 'surrender to science'. It should be understood that, in the cultivation of the fields of inquiry that have come to be known as 'scientific', there is no less need for the exercise of 'judgement', for the recognition of logical categories or the formal distinction among types of problem, for the removal of hypotheses of division in reality, than there is in the pursuit of any other inquiry; it is as speculative and critical, not as 'technical', that work in these fields would be truly scientific. But in fact what we find there is the multiplication of divisions and specializations, the identification of 'method' not with logic but with the use of technical devices, the substitution of a mechanical for a critical apparatus. And it is this narrow, specializing and instrumentalist attitude that has infected the most influential schools of philosophy at the moment, leading them largely to ignore the history of philosophy, the 'classics' of the subject which could provide them with an outlook at once broader and more critical.

The classics of philosophy, as of any other cultural subject, are those works which so fully expound and illustrate objective principles or expose subjective illusions that they have critical application in any age and do not depend on passing fashions. And this can be said particularly of the Greek classics, without which it would be impossible to see the foundation of the main departments of Western thought (politics being an outstanding example), and which are still drawn upon, though in an eclectic manner, even by those who boast of 'starting afresh'. But what, for our present predicament, classical studies in the narrower sense most strikingly bring out is the

---

of individual thinkers, while knowledge of the docrines of individual thinkers and their historical connections can help us to arrive at philosophical truths (to learn philosophy). This conjunct operation of critical factors, leading to fresh discovery and to comprehensiveness of view, illustrates the general principle that the coherent position, the position that 'makes sense', is the one on which all lines of criticism converge.

interdependence of the classical works in all departments of culture, so that the liberally educated man, whatever his leading interest, will range in his studies over the whole classical field. Indeed, the most insidious foe to classicism and the objective outlook is the specialism which cuts some department of culture off from the rest and is therefore antagonistic to that solid core of philosophical criticism which is corrective of any attempt to have one set of critical principles for one subject and a separate set for another, with intellectual chaos where they come into collision. Classicism, in short, stands for the unity of culture against all forms of subjectivism and interestedness, and for the unity, the common principles, of criticism against specialism and *ad hoc* devices—and it is these unities that I take the very existence of this Council[10] to symbolize.

[10] The Australian Humanities Research Council, to which, in the first instance, this paper was addressed (12 November 1959).

5

Socrates as an Educator

I. Socrates and Plato

The manner of his life, and still more the manner of his death, have made Socrates an outstanding figure in the history of European thought and morals. That his doctrine has not till recently been adequately understood is due to the fact that he wrote nothing and that his views, fully and clearly as they are expounded in Plato's dialogues, have been taken to be Plato's own. Owing especially to the work of the late Professor John Burnet during his occupancy (1892 to 1926) of the chair of Greek in the University of St Andrews, it is now possible for us not only to recognize the Greek philosophers as the founders of modern science, but to distinguish and appreciate the contributions of Socrates and Plato to science and general culture.

The supreme importance of Plato is not diminished by the recognition, which his own dialogues enable us to make, of the extent of his indebtedness to Socrates. The marking off of the earlier dialogues as thoroughly Socratic permits of a more careful scrutiny of the later dialogues in which the doctrines of Socrates are either criticized or not referred to at all. It is from these, and most of all from the *Laws*, that, according to Burnet, Plato's position and influence are to be truly estimated. In his posthumously published work, *Platonism*[1] (originally deli-

[1] John Burnet, *Platonism*, University of California Press, Berkeley, 1928.

vered as lectures in the University of California in 1926), Burnet actually claims for Plato a decisive influence on Roman law. 'It is not, in my opinion, too much to say that what we call Roman Law is not so much Roman as Hellenistic, and that it has its origin in the *Laws* of Plato.'

The explanation of this apparently extravagant claim is simple. The Academy, which Plato founded, was not only an institute for scientific research but a school for training rulers and legislators, and it sent out such legislators to a considerable number of Greek states, both during and after Plato's time. Their influence would naturally be in accordance with Plato's ideas of sound politics, and the fact that he spent his last years in drawing up the legislative scheme which is set forth in the *Laws*, shows that he wished the work to be carried on on the same lines. When, at a later date, these Hellenic states came under Roman domination, it was found that the original civil law of Rome was inapplicable to them, and the adaptable Romans solved the difficulty by developing a new system which embodied much of the Academic legislation of the conquered states. It was this system which spread throughout the Empire, while the older Roman law was confined to Rome itself and 'became of less and less importance as time went on'. This, Burnet contends, is the explanation of the extraordinary similarities between Plato's dialogue and what we now call Roman Law.

The educational proposals of the *Laws* are particularly important, as Burnet had previously pointed out in his *Greek Philosophy*,[2] for the estimation of Plato's originality and influence. Burnet lays special emphasis on the scheme of *higher* education elaborated in the dialogue. 'We may easily miss the significance of Plato's proposals as to the education of boys and girls from the age of ten onwards. We must remember that in his day there were no regular schools for young people of that age. They were taken to one teacher for music-lessons and

[2] John Burnet, *Greek Philosophy: Part 1. Thales to Plato*, London, 1914.

to another to be taught Homer, and there was no idea of coordinating all these things in a single building under a single direction with a regular staff of teachers. By founding the Academy Plato had invented the university, and now he has invented the secondary school. In consequence we find such schools everywhere in the Hellenistic period, and the Romans adopted it with other things. That is the origin of the medieval grammar school and of all that has come out of it since.'

This recognition of the practical genius of Plato was not possible to those who regarded the *Republic* as the fine flower of Platonism, and neglected the later dialogues. It may indeed be said that it was at no time a reasonable view that Plato, in order to defend the memory of his master, Socrates, should have written dialogues attributing to him views that he never held. There would have been no reverence or even decent feeling about that. But it was only after the dialogues had been fairly definitely dated that Burnet could satisfactorily show, first, that all the dialogues up to the *Republic* expound a common philosophy; secondly, that, if this is not the philosophy of Socrates, we know next to nothing about his views, since all the alternative versions depend upon material arbitrarily selected from Plato's account; and, finally, that the later dialogues in which, with one explicable exception, Socrates plays no prominent part, expound a *different* philosophy, which is led up to by criticism of the Socratic.

The difference is equally marked in the sphere of education and politics, and in the *Timaeus* we have a definite reference to the shortcomings of Socrates in this regard. The point is, as Burnet puts it, that Socrates 'could paint the picture of an ideal state but could not make the figures move. He is made to confess that he could not, for instance, represent his state as engaged in the struggle for existence with other states; to do that men are required who by nature and training have a gift for practical politics as well as for philosophy.' In a word, Socrates was deficient in the historical sense. He imagined, as the earlier dialogues show, that all social and political problems can be solved on purely ethical grounds, by direct reference to what is good. Plato, on the other hand, saw the impossibility of making progress by the application of an unreal standard of perfection, and the necessity of working with existing political forces. The life and teaching of Socrates showed him, as nothing else could, the opportunism of both the leading Athenian parties and the consequent political bankruptcy of Athens. But he did not despair of the political development of other Greek states, and though his efforts were unsuccessful at the time, they were not, as we have seen, without a considerable later influence.

II. Education and Politics

The uncompromising attitude of Socrates rendered it inevitable that he should come into conflict with the Athenian state, though it was not until Athens was definitely on the decline that his teaching was regarded as a serious danger. Even if the democrats had not suspected that there was an actual connection between Socrates and the aristocratic party, his criticism of the existing form of government, threatened as it was both from within and from without, might well have been regarded as profitable only to their enemies.

This is the natural objection to any unhistorical political doctrine, anarchistic or theocratic, which appeals to an ideal 'rule of right'. The theory of rigid guardianship expounded in the *Republic* and the practical deification of Law in the *Crito* might be taken as decisive indications of the opposition of Socrates to anarchism. But, though there may be a difference in ethical conceptions, there is remarkably little practical or logical difference between the anarchistic and the theocratic positions. All our social and political difficulties will be solved, for the one, if we are governed by the spirit of equality and refrain entirely from oppression, for the other, if we are governed by the representatives of God and refrain entirely from disobedience. Neither view can give us any idea of how such conditions can be satisfied or even approached, how we can promote equality or recognize God's representatives. But each implies that the existing temporal power does not exemplify the rule of right, that it holds its position by oppression or usurpation. And thus both tend to support, and especially to be regarded by the ruling body as supporting, those political forces which are 'in opposition' but are striving to secure domination.[3]

We can see, therefore, that it was natural for the democratic rulers to desire to suppress Socrates. But this is not to say that that desire was to their credit, or that severe criticism of their régime was not called for. Certainly 'Be guided by what is good' is inadequate as a solution of political problems, but a scientific consideration of what sort of life is a good one (and, for that matter, of what constitutes oppression) is not politically and socially valueless. What gave particular force to the Socratic criticism was that the political ideas of the democrats were themselves quite unhistorical. The worshipful Athenian people, the sacred tradition of the city, were just as ideally conceived and reverenced as any metaphysical 'Good' could be. The demonstration of the hollowness of these pretensions may have been historically inadequate and politically negative, but, as far as it went, it was logically sound. And the disinterestedness of Socrates' criticism of the democracy and its leaders, as well as of those professional educators who were called Sophists, made it doubly strong. To teach the youth to accept the customs of the city in which they lived may have been an essential part of the theory and practice of 'getting on', but it implied the existence of interested motives which such teachers were unwilling to reveal.

This fact alone gave Socrates an enormous dialectical advan-

[3] For the sake of simplicity I have passed over the case in which the existing temporal power is itself regarded as representing God. But it is worth noting that such pretensions commonly provoke a religious opposition.

tage; and it was further increased, at his trial, by the existence of a political amnesty. In consequence the real charge of fostering aristocratic sentiments could not be brought, and the teaching of Socrates had to be attacked on religious grounds. Socrates pointed out in his defence that his accusers could give only the vaguest account of what his teaching really was, and he strongly denied that he was a teacher at all, in the sense in which they used the term. 'If you have heard', he says to the judges, 'that I undertake to educate men, and exact money from them for so doing, that is not true; though I think it would be a fine thing to be able to educate men, as Gorgias of Leontini, and Prodicus of Ceos, and Hippias of Elis do.' In fact, if what these Sophists give is education, then Socrates is no educator, and he cannot be rightly accused of corrupting the youth by the inculcation of false doctrines, for he has never given doctrinal instruction to anyone.

But Socrates did not deny, but rather gloried in the fact, that he had striven by example and precept to inculcate the spirit of criticism, to encourage the questioning of received opinions and traditions; and nothing that the Athenians could do, he declared, would prevent his pursuing this task while he lived. 'The unexamined life is not worth living'; to lead such a life is to be in the lowest state of ignorance, ignorant even of one's own ignorance. And therefore he would not cease to call upon the Athenians to give an account of their lives, as the facts of life would compel them to do even if they got rid of him.

The Socratic education begins, then, with the awakening of the mind to the need for criticism, to the uncertainty of the principles by which it supposed itself to be guided. This was utterly opposed to the doctrines of the democrats. What education meant for them is seen in the *Apology*, where Meletus, the leading accuser, describes Socrates as the sole perverter of the youth, while everyone else improves them; and again in the *Meno*, where Anytus, the democratic leader (who was really responsible for the prosecution, but kept in the background because the issue was nominally not political but religious), warns Socrates not to be so free with his criticisms of Athenians and their ways. According to these good patriots, to be educated meant simply to become a good Athenian, and that was brought about by enjoying the society of the respectable citizens of Athens.

Now the position of Socrates is simply that this uncritical acceptance of tradition, this acquiring of Athenian virtue, is no education at all. There is no virtue in being an Athenian, no peculiar and superior Athenian brand of goodness, but goodness is the same wherever it occurs, and what passes as good at Athens may not be really good at all. It requires the most careful scrutiny, and until this process of examination has begun, education has not begun. To see the full force of this criticism, we may substitute Australia for Athens, and imagine Socrates saying, 'You think there is some virtue in being Australian, and that a good Australian is better than a good Greek or Italian, but what you call goodness is just your own ignorance.' Clearly such talk would be infuriating, clearly also it would be very hard to answer; for it would only be by way of afterthought, as a mere 'rationalization', that any suggestion as to what the local virtue consisted in, could be made.

III. Knowledge and Opinion

For Socrates, then, what is fundamental to true education is not tradition but criticism. Tradition itself invites criticism, because it represents certain things as worth while but is unable to give any account of their value. Thus the aim of education is to give an account of things, to find out *the reason why*, and thus put knowledge in the place of opinion. Opinion is all that we get from tradition, all that we get from politicians and Sophists, all that the public, 'the great Sophist', is concerned with. For all these what is current is correct. But what is current is a shifting and uncertain thing, it is not 'tied down by the chain of the cause' (the reason why), and so may leave us in the lurch just when we are surest of it. Opinion may be right but only by accident, and without criticism, without the discovery of reasons, we cannot say whether it is right or wrong. We cannot even say whether we understand a received opinion in the same sense as does its promulgator, or whether, when we apply a tradition to a new case, we are not misinterpreting it. The only test is popular clamour, and that is the least steadfast thing of all.

Thus opinions and traditions change, and change without reason, and yet we continue to follow them. If we want to know what we are doing and thus have real guidance in our lives, we must get a grasp of sound principles; and such principles will be upheld for their own sake, and not because they have been handed on to us. Indeed, for the reasons given, they cannot be handed on but must be arrived at by a man's own thinking. Such thinking may, however, be stimulated by opinions and particularly by questions. Thus we find Socrates, in the *Theaetetus*, claiming the power of bringing men's thoughts to birth by means of this process of questioning, and this is the process of education as far as the educator is concerned. But the really important process is that which goes on in the mind of the pupil, and that is thinking or learning. If the aim of education is to be fulfilled, the Sophistic method of *instruction* must be avoided, and the dialectic method, in which the pupil is led to form his own hypotheses and test them, adopted. Instruction, by discouraging the critical exercise of the pupil's intelligence, prevents the real acquisition of knowledge.

This theory is worked out in connection with the doctrine of reminiscence as expounded in the *Meno* and the *Phaedo*. Under the stimulus of objects of opinion we recall those criteria or standards which alone give the former their meaning, and with which we were directly acquainted in a previous state. Divesting this view of its mythical character, we may say that the question is of finding certain self-explanatory principles, in the light of which we can estimate the transient objects of ordinary life, and thus have settled and organized knowledge. The systematic character of a man's thinking is the test of his progress from opinion to knowledge, as the orderly character of his actions is the test of his progress towards goodness.

Now this implies the ascription, in the Socratic theory, of a certain relative value to opinions and traditions. They may stimulate our search for what is of settled value and thus for an organized way of life. But in themselves they are inadequate, they cannot in the proper sense of the word be *learned*, because they have not been taken up into a self-explanatory system. The first point that Socrates always makes in his criticism of opinions and traditions is their mutually contradictory character. They imply a diversity of principle which is necessarily bad, weak and miserable; the only strong and happy life is the single-minded pursuit of the good. Here we have one of the weak points in the Socratic position, since it implies that all men should function alike. But this does not invalidate the characterization of education as *the finding of a way of life*, as contrasted with the mere acquisition of a number of arts or accomplishments. As tradition may have a relative value, so may the development of a particular aptitude, but it must be made a part of an organized way of life.

We can see from this that Plato's scheme of secondary education owed something to the fundamental conceptions of Socrates. It is also of interest to notice that Socrates, in his criticism of the Sophistic training in accomplishments, was cutting at the root of the modern psychological theory of abilities. Abilities, taken by themselves instead of as part of the general activity of the individual, are falsified and misdirected. The determination of a 'vocation' on the basis of a classification of aptitudes may rightly be called an *external* method of procedure, since the classification can be arrived at only by reference to the occupations that are offered. Thus our modern Sophists, as G. K. Chesterton points out, try to discover what job a man is fit for, instead of asking what way of life is fitting for the man; they 'temper the shorn lamb to the wind'. Similarly, the eugenists desire to breed men for special characteristics, which they consider would be an improvement on existing characteristics, without giving any critical consideration to the notion of improvement or of goodness. 'What's Wrong with the World', as Chesterton puts it in his book with that title,[4] 'is that we do not ask what is right'. We proceed on the basis of notions of improvement, efficiency and fitness, we advocate special tasks, without inquiring what work is really worth doing.

What Socrates stood for, then, against the advocates of 'up-to-date' methods of efficiency and specialization, was coordination or integration of activities. Guidance, he admitted, is possible and desirable, but it must take place in a common and continuous life, and not by any isolated 'test' of capacities, and it must aim at the greatest possible coordination of activities, and not at the isolation and development of some special activity. It is for this reason that the teacher, who has lived and worked with the pupil, is the best judge of what he can do. But to be a judge he requires above all to inquire into what is best, to ask *the reason why*, and not take it for granted that existing demands (opinions) must be satisfied; and in pursuance of this policy he will also encourage the pupil to ask the reason why. In this way real guidance and a really coordinated life are possible. And, if we discount the Socratic overemphasis on ethics, we can still derive from his theories a recognition of the necessity of considering every way of life in its full social and political context. The Socratic view thus finds an interesting modern parallel in the slogan of Lenin, 'Every cook a politician!'

It is true that in the ideal state portrayed in the *Republic* real political understanding is supposed to be confined to the ruling caste. This is due to the way in which Socrates divided knowledge from opinion, to his contention that the former is

[4] G. K. Chesterton, *What's Wrong with the World?*, London, 1910.

concerned with special objects, the forms or standards, instead of simply involving a more critical treatment of the same objects. But this can largely be corrected by means of his own theory of logical coordination. The method Socrates adopts, however, is to allow a certain relative value to opinion and consequently to a life which, though not itself inspired by understanding, obeys the dictates of understanding. In fact, preliminary education precisely takes the form of learning to go about things in the right way, and only after that can we enter on a course of higher education and get to know what makes such actions right.

IV. The Place of Dialectic in Education

The final working out of the educational theory of Socrates is thus to be found in the first and second schemes of education elaborated in the *Republic*. The early training of the guardians (which is all the training given to those who are not fitted for higher study) produces right opinion, or ability and willingness to follow the dictates of those who have knowledge, but does not produce knowledge. Or, to employ the distinction drawn in the *Phaedo*, it cannot give true or 'philosophic' goodness, but only 'popular' (or civic) goodness. 'The former', as Burnet puts it, 'depends on intellect, the latter on habit. It is the former alone that is teachable; for it alone is knowledge, and nothing can be taught but knowledge. The latter is only good at all in so far as it participates in the former. Apart from that it is a shifting and uncertain thing.' That is to say, the early education must be directed by those who have had the later education, and not by those who can themselves lay claim to no more than opinion. There is a logical difficulty in that, if the goodness acquired in the early training really 'participates in' (that is, partakes of the nature of) true goodness, it cannot be a mere matter of habituation but must partake of critical activity as well. The concessions which Socrates makes to 'opinion' are really due to his anti-historical bias, and weaken, instead of strengthening, his critical case. What should be recognized (as Socrates himself has enabled us more clearly to do) are the different factors of guidance and originality, but these should both be present at any stage in the process of education.

The unhistorical character of the theory of early training in right habits appears in the complementary assumptions of a purely imitative faculty in the pupils, their original tendencies being neglected, and of the existence of 'wise and good' educators, whose simple business it is to set up proper models of behaviour, and who are not themselves learning in the educative process. The *Ethics* of Aristotle is based on the same assumptions (being largely derived from the *Republic*), and thus passes over the critical problems of ethics and education. 'Conditions of soul', Aristotle says, 'arise from activities of like character to the conditions.' We become good by doing the right thing, that is, the thing the good man would do under the same circumstances; and therefore he must be there in the first place to tell us what to do, so that we may acquire the habit.

The alternative to this guidance is that we should be subject to the misguiding influence of pleasures and pains. 'It is pleasure that makes us do what is bad, and pain that makes us abstain from what is right. That is why we require to be trained from our earliest youth, as Plato has it, to feel pleasure and pain at the right things. True education is just that.' In his *Aristotle on Education* Burnet goes so far as to say of this that it 'is the best account of the training of character that has ever been given and should be engraved on the heart of every educator.' What it lacks, however, is any explanation of *how* the training takes place, how the affection comes to be transferred from one thing to another—unless the assumption of a general tendency to demand what we have become accustomed to (by having it constantly thrust upon us) is to pass for an explanation. Whereas Plato, in the *Laws*, goes on to take the child's spontaneous activities as of fundamental importance for any training he is to receive, the more rationalistic Socrates and Aristotle appear to regard him as a mere seeking and avoiding mechanism, whose development is determined by what he is allowed to get (or compelled to take).

The theory of habituation, then, is defective precisely in that it neglects the spontaneity of thought which had been emphasized by Socrates in his criticism of opinion or 'what is accepted by all right-thinking men'. We may therefore expect to find a correlative defect in his account of that spontaneity or of higher education. We have seen that the fundamental weakness of his philosophy is its unhistorical character, and this finds its logical expression in the attribution of true reality to certain unchanging 'forms', or ideals, everything changeable being relatively unreal. It is in terms of these forms, Socrates holds, that it is possible to 'give an account' of things. This raises the question of what account can be given of the forms themselves. They cannot each be self-explanatory, or they would be quite unrelated and would not form a system of reality. Accordingly the system itself, or, more precisely, its principle of organization, has to be taken as the one self-explanatory entity; and this is what Socrates calls 'the form of the Good'. It is the one self-sustaining or truly spontaneous thing; and what we call spontaneity in ourselves or in other things is dependent upon it, and exhibits the degree of our or their harmony with it.

But when Socrates is asked to give an account of this 'Good' itself, he can do so only in vague metaphor. This must be so; for if it is explained only by itself, clearly *we* cannot explain it. But in that case all that we are saying, when we postulate its existence, is that there is 'something, we know not what', which is the ultimate explanation of reality. Obviously, in assuming that there is such a thing, we are not entitled to call it good, nor can we derive from what is unknown to us any assurance that some historical thing is good or is better than another. Hence in making his moral distinctions, in saying what should be studied and what should not, Socrates, just like the Sophists, is falling back on opinion. He, too, gives an 'explanation' which is no explanation; he, too, has to depend upon 'what is accepted by all right-thinking men'—only, his right-thinkers are not the same as those of Protagoras and other Sophists.

To show that Socrates was also infected by the Sophistry he criticized is not, however, to take away all value from his criticism or from his theory of higher education. It more especially explains the weakness of his scheme of early education, its moralistic character—particularly exemplified in the unaesthetic treatment of art, which is considered to be purely imitative and to have its value, positive or negative, solely according as it is or is not a good model for the pupils in turn to imitate. This view of art and education is typical of the *mechanical*, or 'external', conceptions which Socrates elsewhere condemned, and which are condemned in the working out of that Dialectic which he regarded as the culmination of the higher education.

The theory of Dialectic itself implies that there can be no set of habits which are entirely in accordance with sound thinking and living, and therefore that habituation cannot be a sound method by itself; for Dialectic requires the unlearning of much that has been previously learned. It may be said, in fact, that there is an element of unlearning in all learning; we acquire new reactions to things by developing and altering old ones. The mind is never a *tabula rasa*, and therefore never merely imitative; but, as Plato recognized in the *Laws*, we have certain tendencies to begin with, and it is only by their exercise that we learn. We learn, that is, by trial and error, or, as in the Socratic theory of criticism expounded in the *Phaedo*, by the formation and testing of hypotheses.

What makes guidance necessary is our tendency to stick to established modes of reaction, in spite of confusions and errors. As education advances, the process of removing confusions becomes more of a deliberate act on the part of the learner. But, whatever be the degree of assistance rendered, the process of clarification involves the breaking up of fixed ideas, the rejection of hypotheses which have hardened into prejudices. Thus 'clearing the mind of cant' is a characteristic of the educative process in general; and Dialectic is simply the theory of the kind of hypotheses it is necessary to reject—those, namely, which would make the prosecution of inquiry impossible, being set above our scrutiny. The most prevalent form of this cant is the 'disabling' of criticism, the treatment of the critic as an ill-disposed person, one who is not worth attending to, *because he criticizes*. Such evasion of the issue is described by the educated as 'illogical', but the pointing out of fallacies of this kind is a very small part of what is involved in Logic or Dialectic. Its full import can be grasped only when we consider it in relation to the most advanced studies, that is, to the sciences.

The special scientist, Socrates contends, uses hypotheses which he does not criticize and of which, in fact, he cannot 'give an account'. They are taken as defining his field of study, and within that field, or using those assumptions, he prosecutes his inquiries and arrives at his conclusions. Thus the mathematician arrives at 'mathematical truths'. But actually there is no mathematical truth, any more than there is an Athenian truth. Fields of study are not cut off from one another but mingle just as peoples do. And to treat each as a separate 'world' is to fall into contradictions. It is the business of Dialectic to show that the supposed 'indemonstrables' and 'indefinables' of the sciences are not indemonstrable or indefinable, but are subject to investigation. Thus all hypotheses implying a division in reality require to be 'destroyed' (or removed).

What this involves is that there is a single logic which applies to all the sciences, a single way of being which all their objects have; we cannot divide reality into higher and lower orders, for the difference and the relation between them would alike be indefinable and indemonstrable. Thus any 'science' which affects to discover powers or faculties which 'make things what they are', or to apply 'laws' to 'phenomena', is guilty of logical error. The Socratic theory of forms itself calls for dialectic criticism. And though Socrates maintains the possibility of finding the 'reason' of these forms in a single ultimate principle, the very assumption of this principle involves a separation (between the ultimate and the relative) which requires to be removed. The application of logic to 'reasons' leads to the conclusion, already obscurely apprehended by the first Ionian philosophers, that any explanation must be on the same level as the thing explained, so that the former in turn can be explained in a similar way.

But the discovery of illogicalities in the theory of Socrates does not affect the fact that he has given a valuable account of the conditions of scientific inquiry. And on this basis we get an important development of his criticism of specialization. Every scientist should be a dialectician, critical of hypotheses and recognizing the continuity of things, since otherwise he will make mistakes in his science and be unable to correct them. In the same way, such activities as teaching and politics should not be regarded as trades or specialities. Every teacher should be an investigator, every politician a thinker. And, since the distinction between the different types of goodness falls to the ground along with the supposition of an unchanging reality behind history, the logical extension of the argument is, as already indicated, that every citizen should be a politician. No one else can do his thinking for him; and the least thinking will lead him to reject the political and social guidance of 'experts' who have no social or political theory. It will readily be seen, for example, that such Sophistic cures for social ills as the encouragement of the 'efficient' and the elimination of the 'unfit' are based on no coordinated or logical view of society, and thus are merely prejudices to be removed.

But this is because society is viewed unhistorically, as a mere field for personal agreements and disagreements, and not as a developing thing. Socrates is wrong in assuming that social issues can be decided on the basis of a general principle of consistency or coordination, and his democratic opponents could rightly say that his proposals must really have had a more special source, must have arisen, that is, from a definite attitude on particular social questions. In general, we can criticize only by reference to beliefs which we definitely hold; otherwise there would be nothing to say for or against any disputed view. And unless this feature of logical criticism is recognized, the Socratic insistence on logic, the setting of criticism against instruction, is misleading. So long as we do not set anything above criticism, we can make progress; but we do so not by having any kind of higher knowledge, but by having opinions and acting on them, that is, by reacting on things which are as historical as ourselves. To have an opinion or belief is to hold something to be true, to be an actual fact, and we cannot make more of it than that; so that there is no place for the Socratic 'knowledge'. When this necessary correction is borne in mind, the position of Socrates can still be seen to be of real value in pointing the way to the discovery of educational and political truths—namely, by critical activity in science and politics.

6

Lectures on the Educational Theories of Spencer and Dewey

I. Utilitarianism and Education

It is common for writers on education to deal with what it shall or ought to be rather than with what it is, just as they often consider education as an instrument of social improvement in general. The modern outlook is a reforming one which assumes utilitarianism, the view that there are common human ends or things which it is natural for people to pursue. These ends are summed up in the conception of 'happiness', and it is felt that only by some distortion of human nature would people have any ends other than the common happiness. More specifically, the modern outlook assumes that if people were correctly informed, that is, thoroughly acquainted with the facts of the case, they could not under any circumstances pursue anything other than the common happiness. The theory is that nature dictates an end for humanity, and that the solution for any social problem consists simply in the correction of deviations by the giving of exact information in place of mistaken ideas.

That view is one ingredient in Benthamism; and it also recurs again and again in thinkers who may not be explicit Benthamites but who do press the claim of what they call 'science' in the determination of human thinking and living.

For example, in Spencer and Huxley we have the assumption that knowledge of the facts prescribes a certain policy. They fail to see that, in telling us how certain things go on, a science does not tell us what to do: that it does not tell us what ends to pursue nor, if a number of different objects of human pursuit are being considered, that one of these is better than or preferable to another.

If there are in fact a number of forms of human behaviour other than the pursuit of general happiness, then it is quite unscientific to say that they are unnatural and that only the pursuit of general happiness is in accordance with human nature. That is simply to deny the facts. If we attack the matter from another side and ask what general happiness or utility may be, we find that it has no positive content. We find the quite arbitrary assumption that, because each person has ends, that is, things that would satisfy him or would constitute his happiness, people in general have an end which would constitute the general happiness.

It is possible in relation to any person to form the conception of 'his getting all that he wants', but it is not the case that the objects of his various desires add up to one, so that he has a distinct desire 'to get all that he wants'. That each man pursues his own happiness is obvious only in the uninformative sense that he pursues whatever he pursues. Again, if there were a conflict among his demands, it could not be resolved by any ruling 'desire' to have all his demands satisfied. So, it is not possible for *any* man to pursue the general happiness, if this means the satisfying of all demands. Even if there were no conflict among his own demands, there would always be conflict between the demands of different men, and no way of satisfying them as a whole.

I think that something positive can be found behind the vague notion of happiness, and something that is important for social theory. But the more precisely we define happiness the less plausible it is to say that it is an object aimed at. I consider that the place of aims in explaining human behaviour is greatly exaggerated, but if we are dealing with the kinds of things aimed at, it is necessary to recognize the diversity of these, and not to treat happiness as the one thing aimed at in an unqualified way.

Since the theory of evolution is commonly taken, quite unjustifiably, to prescribe a certain end for us, the utilitarian position is stimulated by evolutionary ideas. In fact, Spencer's 'evolutionism', which takes evolution to be the unfolding of reality as a whole, favours the assumption of progress, that is, the assumption that improvement is the natural thing in education and in society as a whole. I take this to be the forcing of certain demands on the facts. It is an assumption that is certainly not buttressed by any exact view of evolution. But it is an assumption which arises naturally enough with respect to education, because it will be readily conceded that a person is not being educated unless he is progressing, that is, unless he is advancing in knowledge. However, the fact that this or that individual is acquiring knowledge and developing in other capacities does not imply that society as a whole is advancing, nor that within it subjects of study are advancing, that is, acquiring greater exactness and covering a wider range of phenomena. It is clear that there would always be junior members of society being educated, even if there were retrogression in human knowledge generally.

Spencer is an example of the class of thinkers who start, not from the conception of what education is, but from the consideration of what it should be or could be made to be. It may be suggested that we are forced into some such position as this because we can find no common character, other than something exceedingly general, of the various things that are called education, or of the activities within educational institutions. Yet if there is a problem about the variety of things called education, it is not to be solved arbitrarily by putting forward our personal notion of what is desirable and trying to get a scheme in which this will be the dominant consideration. This is just what Spencer does, though it is disguised by the contention that 'respecting the true measure of value, as expressed in general terms, there can be no dispute'.[1]

Spencer's initial contrast between the ornamental and the useful has the same suggestion that there will be universal agreement with his criterion once people stop merely following the fashion in education. Concerning what 'determines the character of our education', he says, 'Not what knowledge is of most real worth, is the consideration; but what will bring most applause, honour, respect—what will most conduce to social position and influence—what will be most imposing.' (p. 4).

For Spencer the reference to the ornamental is meant to be depreciatory, to indicate something that is being valued and pursued in an irrational way. But if we make a contrast between the useful and the ornamental, it is arguable that the latter would be the more important or would have more weight attached to it, because we commonly mean by a useful thing something which has 'instrumental value', that is, something that we want because it leads to something else, to something, namely, which we want just for its own sake. It is impossible to maintain that *all* objects of human demand are 'useful' in this instrumental sense. We should have to admit that some are 'ornamental' in the sense that we demand them for no other reason than that we like them.

We cannot, then, determine on the basis of utility alone what education, or any other form of social activity, is to be. We should have, in the end, to revert to the 'ornamental', at least in the sense of what is wanted for no reason outside itself. An educational system could not be purely utilitarian, or satisfy no demand other than that for the useful, unless the meaning of 'useful' were extended to embrace both what we want because of what it leads to and what is wanted just for itself. But if Spencer made this extension he would do away

[1] Herbert Spencer, *Education: Intellectual, Moral and Physical*, 1911, Thinker's Library, 3rd. Impression, 1938, p. 7. (First published 1903.)

with any obvious antithesis between the ornamental and the useful.

As Spencer develops his theory, it appears that he wants to uphold a conception of general human utilities, that is, of things that are in general demand or are useful for any purpose whatever. It is these, he thinks, that should determine human conduct and education. No doubt such things as food, shelter and clothing could be regarded as general human utilities, in the sense that all people, or practically all, require them for any life that they may follow. But it does not follow that these common utilities would be regarded as more important than the interests which distinguish one life from another; and once we recognize, not merely the distinction, but the conflict among such interests, we can see that this reacts on the common utilities. Some interests, in maintaining themselves, would deprive others of those general requirements. The mere fact of wanting the same kinds of thing would not lead to agreement between people on the supply of these. It may lead to competition and to disagreement as to their allocation. This means that general utility would not serve as a criterion for evaluating educational systems, or as a basis for establishing a system which will avoid conflict of interests.

Spencer's admission that education is pursued in directions other than those which his notion of utility would prescribe points to the conflict of interests which is the stumbling-block for his theory. He is fond of illustrating his complaint that in our education the ornamental overrides the useful by referring to people who exhibit, for effect, tags of classical knowledge that are quite useless for practical life. His antithesis between the ornamental and the useful obscures the sort of case that may be made for classical education quite apart from any appeal to usefulness in practical affairs. This kind of education, it may be argued, leads to a special sort of mentality that would be recognized in later life by the kind of judgement it exercises.

According to Spencer, the chief question to be asked in determining what education is to be is 'how to decide among

the conflicting claims of various subjects on our attention'
(Spencer, *Education*, p. 6). There is no dispute, he maintains,
about the criterion to be applied in determining this; it is the
bearing that the subject has on life, and ultimately its importance for the question 'how to live', that is, the place it has in
the system of 'complete living':

To prepare us for complete living is the function which education
has to discharge; and the only rational mode of judging of an educational course, is, to judge in what degree it discharges such function
(p. 7).

There are two lines of objection to such a position. First,
Spencer is including in education any training whatever, and
the acquisition of any power that the human infant is not born
with but comes to possess. Secondly, by means of the notion
of complete living, Spencer is upholding the dogma that these
acquisitions add up to a single acquisition. This, like utilitarian
doctrines generally, overlooks qualitative distinctions and
oppositions, and attempts to put things on a purely quantitative basis, a basis of more and less. It assumes, in other words, a
common measure of any two forms of human activity.

Filling out the notion of complete living, Spencer goes on to
'classify, in the order of their importance, the leading kinds of
activity which constitute human life.' He sets these out as:

(1) Those activities which directly minister to self-preservation;
(2) Those activities which, by securing the necessaries of life, indirectly minister to self-preservation;
(3) Those activities which have for their end the rearing and discipline of offspring;
(4) Those activities which are involved in the maintenance of proper
social and political relations;
(5) Those miscellaneous activities which fill up the leisure part of
life, devoted to the gratification of the tastes and feelings (p. 8).

It is only with the fifth class that Spencer approaches the

appraisal of the variety of ways of living or forms of organization which exist in the modern industrial society whose educational system he wishes to reform. Activities of all five classes
are carried on by adults in that society, and would be assessed
in many cases by reference to some form of social living which
was taken as the thing of major importance in 'human life'.
Spencer, however, wants some 'rational' scale of importance.
He thinks that provision for any such special 'cause' to which
men may devote themselves must be postponed to provision
for the social life which 'makes possible' any such special form
of social living.

Spencer presents his order of importance as rational because
it follows the order in which the classes of activity make one
another possible, but the temporal order he proposes is open to
criticism at various points. It may well be maintained that 'the
family comes before the State in order of time' (p. 9), but does
this mean that it makes social life possible? In this case Spencer
is dealing with the order in which two institutions appeared in
the history of the human race. However, he offers no such
justification for the temporal precedence of the second class to
the third. Here he refers to the order in which certain activities
appear in the individual human being. He says that 'speaking
generally, the discharge of the parental functions is made
possible only by the previous discharge of the industrial ones'
(p. 9). In the history of the human race the precedence of some
type of work to some type of family might perhaps be made
good, but postponing parental responsibilities to 'earning
one's living' is more an ideal of bourgeois society than a fact of
life. In any human community which persists through successive generations, activities of the first three classes would
always go on together. We might envisage a group of human
beings which attended to preservation of its adult members
and did nothing towards rearing the children, but unless a
group did take on the third class of activities it would not
continue as a tribe or people.

The most plausible part of Spencer's theory of the temporal

order in human activities is that leisure activities appear later than social and political activities. Clearly there are particular types of cultural activity, to use a less vague description, which need not exist in a given society. There could, then, be a society without these particular activities, though they could not exist without society. But this does not mean that the class of cultural activities would *as a whole* come later in time than the class of social activities, or that there could be a society without *some* activities of a cultural kind.

We might agree with Spencer that 'a considerable development' of such things as music, poetry and painting is 'impossible without a long-established social union' (pp. 9–10) and yet question whether there can be a society entirely lacking in such activities. But what is in any case quite obvious is that there is no possibility of the mere continuance of society as such. It is always a question of a society of a certain kind. Since it is only with respect to the fifth class of activities that Spencer indicates how different ways of living could give rise to various kinds of society, this class might be taken, on his showing, to be the most important for any concrete handling of the question of the survival or continuance of societies. In the case of the other four classes, Spencer deals with activities common to most human beings without reference to variations (for example, in their manner of obtaining or distributing food). His treatment of these other classes of activity is concerned almost exclusively with merely formal considerations that seem to be relevant to the survival of society in general but have little or no bearing on the question of what types of social living are surviving or struggling for survival.

When Spencer considers the respective places in an educational scheme of his fourth and fifth classes of activity, he says: 'That part of human conduct which constitutes good citizenship, is of more moment than that which goes out in accomplishments or exercise of the tastes; and in education preparation for the one must rank before preparation for the other' (p. 10). This exemplifies what may be called the utilitarian view that we can make provision first for the mere continuance of society and then for the quality of what is to continue by subsequently providing for the flourishing of special sorts of activity within society.

The question is a general one but it is frequently complicated by individualistic assumptions. The struggle for existence as applied to man is viewed as a struggle among individual men instead of as a struggle between ways of living or types of organization, that is, special activities which might cease to exist though men go on living. If the problem is that of the survival of a particular kind of culture, the survival of a mere aggregate of men does not offer a solution. It cannot be assumed that just because they survive they are capable of devoting themselves to a particular culture. At any time there are competing forms of social organization or types of social living, and some of these (under given conditions) may be unable to maintain themselves. No policy could somehow provide for all possible societies or all possible forms of social living. The satisfaction of the needs of one way of life means the non-satisfaction of the needs of another.

There will, of course, be general conditions common to a number of actual and possible ways of living, and consequently certain problems common to the sorts of training that are current in them. For example, in the acquisition and transmission of any special skill or power, in the carrying on of any special activity from generation to generation, there will be general problems such as the getting of food. However, it is the points of distinction, not the common features of ways of living, that must be regarded as most important in relation to education.

It is only recently, following the line of thought represented by Spencer and Huxley, that education has been taken to cover the development of all powers, whatever they may be, which the child acquires or is not born with. Earlier the word 'education' was regularly confined to the development of activities in Spencer's fifth class, and particularly to intellectual activities.

What Spencer presents as *the* rational system of education for any society whatsoever is really a particular kind of training for a particular kind of society.

At the present time there is an opposition, within education and educational theory, between two tendencies which may be called 'utilitarian' and 'cultural'. If there is within education the tendency towards the sort of system which Spencer presents as necessary for complete living, this educational tendency may conveniently be called a 'utilitarian' one in contrast to the cultural, so long as we remember that this tendency will not represent all that utilitarian theory regards as desirable. I should argue that the utilitarian tendency within educational and social theory—and it is both powerful and widespread at the present time—does amount to the flourishing of a particular kind of social activity or organization in opposition to other kinds.

Utilitarian theorists, however, discount such qualitative distinctions and oppositions, and within educational theory this has some curious results. Thus, Spencer not only makes education cover all acquisitions but also contends that these acquisitions are actually parts of one significant whole, complete living, by reference to which it is possible to decide how much attention is to be given to each part. Things as different as physical training and literary training are treated as just two parts of a common substance of which the pupil can get a certain amount. Again, in some theories the denial of differences leads to claims of an egalitarian kind being made on education, that is, to the notion that education should be uniform in character and confined to the sort of training which the great majority can encompass.

Spencer's treatment of education in the first essay is largely determined by two principles, namely that education covers all acquisitions and that those acquisitions are most important which have most to do with simple survival. It is these that enable him to argue that the most important ingredient of education is science. Of course, if we identified science with knowledge, science would embrace all parts of an intellectual training, but Spencer is thinking particularly of physical science. He takes physical science to be the model and foundation of all science or all knowledge.

Leaving the major objections to this view for later consideration, we may note that it leads to some quite grotesque results when the criterion of 'usefulness for living' is employed in the choice of educational material. There was great emphasis, especially in the late nineteenth century, on physiology or 'the laws of health'. As appears even more clearly in Huxley than in Spencer, it was held that we have to know the laws of nature in order to live in accordance with them.

That position is subject to criticism in two ways. First, laws of nature are not prescriptions but descriptions. More exactly, they describe the ways in which things go on whether anyone is acquainted with or desires these particular ways of proceeding or not. Secondly, in so far as we can pursue a policy, this policy is not dictated by a law of nature or by our knowledge of such a law, that is, by the sort of thing in accordance with which we are said to choose. If alternative courses of action are possible, then no one of them follows from a given law of nature. Otherwise there would not be any alternatives. The view that when we know the laws of nature there is only one course of action that we can pursue is bound up with an additional and confused doctrine of utilitarianism. This is the doctrine that there are certain settled or natural ends of human behaviour, and that the only way in which knowledge can influence our conduct is by giving us information about what are, and what are not, means to these settled ends. If we do not make that assumption and simply look at the facts, then we find people utilizing the same information for entirely diverse ends.

Spencer, however, keeps to utilitarianism. He uses the notion of complete living as the common end of action in general. Thus he brings into a single class everything that we could possibly pursue, and suggests that the question is only one of getting more or less of such a totality. He ignores the fact that attainment of some of those ends prevents the attainment of others. He ignores qualitative differences and conflicts. He does admit that his 'complete living' is an ideal, something which we can never quite attain. At the same time, he holds that the problem is to get as much of it as we can, so that our choices are of more or less, not this or that. Thus, the assumption is—and this is paralleled in such current notions as 'welfare'—that there is a common substance of which people can get a certain amount, and the more they can get the better.

From this point of view all kinds of training are lumped together as education. The literary and critical training, which I should take to be the distinctively educational training, and, for example, physical training are taken to be merely different parts of one training. They are taken to present different parts of a common material instead of quite distinct kinds of training. We may acknowledge that anyone who is being educated in the literary sense must also have some kind of physical training or at least physical development. However, there is no order of precedence such as Spencer suggests; the two kinds of training would run concurrently. Again, there is no fundamental reason for taking the two in a single institution; in fact, even in modern schooling they are largely developed separately. The reasons for their being taken together as much as they are, are political and financial rather than educational.

It is in terms of a general utilitarian outlook that the doctrine of the unity of all subject-matters and of the materials of all forms of training has developed, and along with that comes the doctrine of educational uniformity (see the chapter 'Democracy in Education' in Dewey's book). This is the view that education means the sort of training that is suitable for everyone, that is, the training of everyone as a member of society. The latter doctrine will quite naturally be adopted if we have set out from the former. If there is a common material of which any particular person can get a certain amount, then there seems to be no reason for giving more of it to one person than to another. The requirement seems to be for the same treatment and the same share to all who are being trained for the same kind of life. On this theory that means all people.

On the other hand, if we recognize differences in training and the different sorts of life that are going to emerge from training, then the notion of equality no longer applies. We cannot say that so much training of the kind A is equal to so much training of the kind B. In so far as the slogan 'education for democracy' implies this uniformity we should have to say, I think, that it is opposed to education in the sense of a literary and critical training. In other words, if universal education means training in what the great majority can be trained in, then I suggest that this means depriving of a special cultural training those who are peculiarly capable of it. It has been said with some justice that social and financial conditions prevent some people who are suitable for this type of training from getting it, but this problem would not be solved by giving everyone the same education of a mediocre level.

II. Subjects and their 'Value'

Having set up his scale of 'importance', Spencer thinks that the greatest attention should be paid to the most important, within the limits of our resources. This means that what he takes to be the least important would have little chance of flourishing—and this is something which is actually the case—in those so-called 'educational' systems which follow a Spencerian or 'scientific' line. Persisting with his notion of 'complete living', the unity which I have argued does not exist, he says that 'the worth of any kind of culture, as aiding complete living, may be either necessary or more or less contingent.' He distinguishes here between (i) 'knowledge of intrinsic value', (ii) 'knowledge of quasi-intrinsic value', and (iii) 'knowledge of conventional value'.

He takes the truths of science to belong to the first class because 'they will bear on human conduct ten thousand years hence as they do now' (Spencer, *Education*, p. 11). Strangely enough, these truths have *intrinsic* value because of their bearing on *something else*.

In the second class he puts acquaintance with Latin and Greek. This knowledge has quasi-intrinsic value because it is useful for a certain time or under certain conditions, but not always or everywhere. 'The extra knowledge of our own language, which is given by an acquaintance with Latin and Greek, may be considered to have a value that is quasi-intrinsic: it must exist for us and for other races whose languages owe much to these sources; but will last only as long as our languages last' (p. 11). Once more the criterion is quantitative—the question is of the range of cases in which a thing will be useful—while qualitative distinctions are neglected.

Admittedly defenders of classical education very often use arguments of this type. They defend the classics for their instrumental value, for example, their usefulness in deepening our understanding of English, and would supplement this point presumably by referring to the use of English for social communication. But while this is a weak sort of argument, it does not follow that we should discount the conclusion that classical education is valuable. It may well happen that people have not thought out the reasons for their practices and ways of defending them, but have just carried on with a feeling of the rightness of what they are doing. Then they fall into confusion when they are asked to make out a case, especially to people who have not the same interests. It should also be remembered that any such justification must stop at some point. It must stop at an interest in, a determination to carry on, certain types of activity irrespective of what other activities they might promote. Thus it might be quite impossible to bring home to a utilitarian the value of the classics; and a person who is forced to attempt it might be unable to avoid arguing badly, making out a poor sort of case, just because he is expressing himself in terms of his opponent's values.

At the same time, we should notice that the support of classicism in education does not imply that the person who is carrying on classical education is doing it well, or in such a way as to bring out the real importance of the classics. There is no such thing as a foolproof curriculum. The so-called 'classicist' often proceeds in a pedantic fashion. In fact, I should say that this has been partly the *result* of attack from the scientific side. The classics teacher may become narrow and hidebound, following certain customary lines without having any large view of education or the place of classics in education. But it may still be the case that there is a real defence of classical education which such people are unable to state, and which in any case would have no appeal to the anti-classicist. (The assumption that anyone should be able to present and understand the case for classicism is an example of the confusion introduced by vulgar notions of democracy. It has its analogue in the assumption that any issue should be intelligible to any voter.)

Study of the classics is essential to the continuance of the classical outlook, that is, the type of activity and the general view of things which are deposited in the classic tongues. Such study enables us to recover and participate in this outlook more fully than we could from our own language alone and, indeed, helps us to grasp the cultural content of our own language also. It is a question of *content*. It is no argument at all against the educational importance of the classical outlook that it is not universally accessible: that it would not be accessible when the present languages have changed or disappeared, or is not accessible in countries where there is no continuity with classical culture, no Graeco-Roman tradition. Equally, it is no argument against the educational value of classics if it can be established that classical education must remain inaccessible to a considerable section of the population, whether this is on the grounds of limitation of resources or those of personal incapacity. These considerations would not affect the contention, in whatever way that general contention can be supported, that entry into the classical heritage is essential to education in any distinctive sense, that is, the development of criticism or judgement, as contrasted with training in general.

In his third class, 'knowledge of conventional value', Spencer is concerned with those parts of current educational practice or curriculum which merely confer a certain social distinction on people without adding to their knowledge. Certain types of 'education' carry a reputation, and people want to say that their children have been to such and such a school etcetera, even though with respect to *content* this is of no importance. Here Spencer assumes that his own criteria for importance of content must be universally accepted. He fails to recognize that people did treat these elements of educational practice or curriculum as an essential part of education quite independently of any question of snobbery, and that it was for this reason that such subjects were brought into the curriculum. He either misses or ignores the implication that certain people did not share his view of education, his conception of general utility or 'complete living' and the unity of all subject-matters and of training in them.

Spencer is making the utilitarian assumption that there is a general standard and a general order of the usefulness of things which people can be brought to accept, that differences of opinion on these matters are due merely to lack of information, and that once we diffuse the correct information everyone will be in agreement. As against this, I have been arguing that people live qualitatively different lives and in accordance with that fact have different ends or are seeking different things, so that even if they received the same information they would use it in different ways.

Taking Spencer's own example, the teaching of history, we find him arguing not against the presence in the curriculum of the subject history, but against the way in which the subject is taught, namely, as a 'mere tissue of names and dates and dead unmeaning events' (Spencer, *Education*, p. 11). This, he argues, has only conventional value. People are made to feel inferior if they do not know these things. But knowledge of them, he says, 'has not the remotest bearing on any of our actions' (p. 11). In the same chapter he goes on to maintain that history should be taught in a different fashion, namely, in such a way as to give knowledge of the life of peoples and of major constitutional issues and political struggles, such as that between Church and State, in the transition to the modern period.

It seems clear to me that that sort of thing simply cannot be learned by children. If they are given material which purports to cover that ground, then they will be learning it in a merely conventional fashion, that is, as something remembered but not understood. While historical study may be of little value if it remains at the level of names and dates, there is no doubt that that sort of knowledge is of value as a foundation, providing pegs on which later and fuller knowledge can be hung. The same is true of old-fashioned geography, of just becoming acquainted with the various land masses, rivers, towns, etc. Though even these 'mere facts', as they might be called, can be of interest to children in the early stages, history in particular should be, and was in the old-fashioned system, treated in a literary way or as a part of literary study, namely, in the form of stories of a mildly moral description. Such a treatment would of course involve some distortion, but that is inevitable in the early stages and in any case it would be much less than in a treatment of the subject along the lines proposed by Spencer. Spencer, like others in his movement, is putting far too much emphasis on what is called 'the life of the people' as contrasted with the outstanding achievements in culture of the various periods. It is grasping these achievements that is the important thing in such studies as history. The study of 'the common life' of a period would be as dull and useless as the most pedantic course on names and dates.

For Spencer education is not literary but scientific. It will be concerned with what belongs to his first sort of knowledge,

'knowledge of intrinsic value'. The scientific character of education, considered in a very narrow way, is its important character. What we may note, first of all, is that there is confusion or failure of discrimination, on Spencer's part, between two quite different sets of considerations which are involved in his list of the leading kinds of activity that constitute human life. On the one hand, there are the considerations connected with the second kind of activities (those which indirectly minister to self-preservation) where, since it is a question of 'getting a living', science would be more important than literature because it is vocationally more useful. On the other hand, there are considerations relating to the subjects themselves—in particular, the argument that the study and appreciation of literature is itself a scientific process, so that it is only in so far as science, and specifically physical science, enters into our knowledge of the arts that we really do know them at all.

The latter type of argument, though I believe it to be open to serious objections, at least needs careful treatment, but it is to the former considerations that our scientific educators always come back. They are either openly pressing for or smuggling in the requirements for making a living. This, on the face of it, has little to do with a real advance in understanding, with the progress of subjects and the development of power of judgement.

Spencer exaggerates the relevance to education of his second leading kind of activity, activities which indirectly minister to self-preservation. Hence he tends to evaluate education in terms of its vocational effect, that is, its effect on the way in which the pupil is eventually going to make his living. There may be fruitful interaction between economic organization and science, but this does not mean that trade should become an integral part of education; in fact, that would make the interaction less fruitful. While a general education might facilitate a person's entry into his trade by strengthening his ability to deal with its problems, that does not mean that these problems must form an integral part of a general education. Both Spencer and Huxley at least sometimes argue on the principle that if there is anything we cannot get on without then that should form part of general education; whereas such a thing might well remain the concern of specialists who have their special training in institutions attached to the trade in question.

Huxley, for example, in *Science and Education*, finding that medical students are handicapped by lack of knowledge of physics and chemistry when they enter their medical course, argues from that that physics and chemistry should form part of the general schooling. Actually, it might be a reason for extending the medical course, as has been done since Huxley's time, or, though this is more doubtful, for having special schools for those intending to take up the medical profession, but it is no argument for making everyone study physics and chemistry. If the content of education were to be determined on such grounds, then education would be an affair of bits and pieces. It would contain at least as much that is of merely nominal value as the most pedantic schooling to which Spencer objects. To take some further illustrations: it might be said that society could not get on without some study of military science being undertaken, but that would not imply that educated people must have studied military science; or, again, we might attach great social importance to the work of the sanitary engineer, but would not on that account call him an educated man.

In general, Spencer and Huxley are emphasizing externals, things we might regard as useful for whatever kind of life we wanted to lead, and not things that are inherent in ways of living themselves. It is from the latter point of view that an essentially literary training, as against an essentially scientific training, is to be supported, namely, as helping to form a power of judgement, a sense of values. This will be an integral part of the person's subsequent way of life; indeed, it will affect all parts of his life.

In this connection both Spencer and Huxley seem to think that science, what we may call 'the knowledge of nature', lays down lines of action for us. They seem to think that there is a distinction between living according to nature and living in opposition to nature, and that science enables us to do the former. Here we may, first, argue that there is no such thing as living in opposition to nature (and, as a side point, that if there were such a thing we might prefer it to living according to nature), or that any way in which we live and act exemplifies certain laws, certain regular sequences. Secondly, as far as we may be said to adopt policies, as far as we have a choice of pursuing this line or that, science will not tell us which line to pursue. If we know that A produces B, then we may use that knowledge in connection with a policy of either promoting B or of hindering B.

Spencer tries, in particular, to treat art in this way, that is, as something grounded in natural science. He acknowledges verbally that this science does not give a complete account of art, and that science alone will not make an artist. Still he is contending not merely for the possibility of a scientific theory of artistic activity and of aesthetic character, but for science as giving us a criticism of art, giving us something that it is essential for the artist to know, or, at the very least, for the view that better science makes better art.

In the course of his argument he takes up positions that are certainly not justified by the sciences on which he is drawing for guidance. He adopts, for example, what is sometimes called a 'realistic' but would better be called a 'naturalistic' view of art, namely, that art represents life, and that the more exact the representation the better the work so that a sculptor will be the better for knowing physiology and, in particular, for knowing the conditions of human balance (Spencer, *Education*, p. 38). This representationalist view of art is certainly common enough, but it has also been strongly contested. Specifically, we find a formalist view as against the naturalistic; and it would be quite impossible to settle that controversy on physiological grounds, or by appeal to the physical sciences in general.

Again, Spencer will not declare outright that a science, say the science of human speech, will give a complete account of poetry. Nevertheless he holds that the difference between good and bad poetry amounts to that between the poet's observing and his not observing the conditions of excited human speech (pp. 39–40); that is, it is a question of how human beings would express themselves in a given situation. He is assuming, as before, that when we appreciate anything, when we say 'how good this is', we mean 'how like this is to life, how this reminds us of things we are acquainted with'. This would make poetry simply a part of science, or of knowledge, and not an independent thing at all.

That is not to say that poetry, in particular, cannot be an adjunct to science or that there could not be a poetic element in scientific work itself. Indeed, as Spencer suggests, poetry and art generally can awaken us to the realization of what we overlook in ordinary observation, and this sort of inspiration is also characteristic of scientific discovery (pp. 41–2). At the same time, this inspiration is not to be attained by adopting the standpoint of naturalism, that is, by using the criterion of likeness or resemblance. The point which Spencer overlooks in his account of poetry is that ordinary human communication, whether excited or not, is commonly concerned with utilities, that is, with proceeding to certain settled ends in accordance with a conventional set of values.

III. Education as Aesthetic

As against simply taking things for granted because they are customary, one of the main things that art does is to disengage some character of things which is obscured or ignored in customary activities. This point can be illustrated in the case of the visual arts by the expression, 'restoring the innocence of the eye', which implies that the artist uses the senses otherwise than in subordination to predetermined tasks or attends to what is of no use for what we are habitually concerned to do or to bring about (see my essay, 'Art and Morality').[2] This does not mean that the natural powers of apprehension of children are necessarily of an advanced aesthetical character; it refers rather to the limitation which taking things to be means to certain ends imposes on anyone's powers of apprehension.

This raises the general question of objectivity, that is, of an interest in things themselves, independently of special purposes, or of what things might be said to be *for* and of what they could be *used* for. This interest in things themselves, and how they work, I take to be characteristic of the educated man, the man who is not shackled by the assumptions current in his society or group. The power of seeing things objectively is not a mere passivity or receptivity. It requires a criticism of principles if only because all of us have a tendency to fall into mere custom and uncritical living: indeed, we all have up to a point to consider utilities, that is, those matters that Spencer regarded as the most important, and we inevitably have routine activities. So, our interest in objectivity will also have to work its way through obstacles in ourselves and others.

This line of argument, this recognition of the limitations under which education must work, is in accordance with the *pluralistic* view I have been taking against Spencer. This is the view that there is no common denominator of a single person's interests, let alone of the interests of a group, and consequently there is nothing that can be called a training for life or 'complete living', though there is still the opposition between education conceived in Spencer's terms of 'complete living' (utilitarian education) and education in the special sense that I have been supporting (liberal education).

To consider that distinction further, we may notice the importance of aesthetic considerations for education. (Spencer

---

[2] Chapter 11 in this collection (Ed.).

has particular chapters on moral and political education, but none on aesthetic education.) My contention is that education as such (that is, liberal education) is aesthetic; and that, allowing for the confused and narrow way in which 'taste' is commonly spoken of, we can still refer to education as a training in taste or, using the broader term which we find in Arnold, a training in judgement. We are apt to think of judgement especially as a power of discrimination, but it should be said also to involve a power of association or a sense of connection, that is, of the structure or build-up of things. If we adopt a formalistic or structural view in aesthetics, this point would reinforce the conception of training in judgement as aesthetic training.

We have in these terms an opposition between the conception of education as literary and the conception of it as scientific; where, however, the notion of 'science' is a narrow one, that is, of an especially utilitarian or operational kind. Matthew Arnold, in *Literature and Dogma*, insists on the distinction between literary and scientific matters. He considers the latter to be matters on which we can get a clear and direct line of argument and where, in particular, we can have a quite clear grasp of the conceptions we are working with. In the former, however, he holds that we are still groping towards conceptions in which to express our experience, and we only distort or obscure the subject-matter if we try to express it in rigid scientific terms. Arnold thinks that this is what happens in religious matters. That is, when people develop a theology or metaphysic, namely, doctrines of First Cause, *ens realissimum*, etcetera, they are trying to set up a rigid science of what we are not yet able to treat in that manner; and in professing to be clear and positive, they are not merely failing to convey real information, but are hampering the ordinary religious consciousness in its tentative and literary or poetic treatment of what are quite real facts of experience. Thus, he says that Hebrew thought is badly represented by speaking of the Lord as a distinct, personal being with exactly definable characteristics, where a better translation would be 'the Eternal'; something no doubt vaguely conceived, but conceived as having the character of lasting or persisting and the function of being something not ourselves that makes for righteousness.[3]

But Arnold is not entitled to assume that there is this difference of subject-matters at all; that there is any subject-matter that is quite clear-cut and definite, and in regard to which we do not have to recognize the tentativeness of many of our conceptions and the need for a constant criticism of conceptions. The exactness of those sciences, especially modern mechanical science, which are assumed to be quite clear and definite, is a spurious exactness. It is an exactness of a rationalistic sort which amounts to paring away differences, or ignoring inconvenient characters of things, as, for example, in the doctrine of primary and secondary qualities. In other words, it consists in a reduction to 'elements'. This is really a treatment of things simply as subject to certain types of operation, namely, those that we are especially taken up with or that are particularly relevant to some line of scientific activity. While it might be easier to see the absurdity of the reduction method in social science, I suggest that this is really the position in all science: a clarity and exactness are assumed, which do not really exist.

In all science—and especially in physical science, because it is here that the point is commonly overlooked—there is the need for a constant criticism of conceptions. This does not occur in physical science. There is at long intervals some sort of revolution in conceptions, an alteration of general terminology or fundamental ideas. But such revolutions do not clear things up to any great extent, because they are still primarily concerned with certain possible human operations on the subject-matter, though perhaps different ones from those with which earlier scientists were concerned. What is needed for the soundest grasp of the subject-matter is not this

---

[3] Matthew Arnold, *Literature and Dogma*, Ch. 1.

occasional house-cleaning, but a criticism that goes along with inquiry all the time, that is, the exercise of that judgement which Arnold has especially associated with literary matters.

It is perhaps most notably in physical science that this spurious exactness is to be found, but it also occurs in social science, specifically in the doctrine of utilitarianism, namely, in the assumption of a common measure of all objects of human pursuit. This assumption has a commercial side that could be associated with the tendency to give all such objects a greater or less money price, and thus to consider them all quantitatively comparable.

This spurious exactness is carried over into economics in operations with such quantities, for example, in finding the 'total value' of a set of commodities by adding together the price of each, even though, since they do not all come on the same market, the notion of 'the sum of their values' has no real meaning; that is, there is no specific demand for all of them taken together. No doubt, the sort of operation in question goes with the belief that all markets are ultimately parts of one market or that there is a general exchange system to which any particular exchange belongs. This belief is involved in the notion of 'perfect capitalism' and underlies the Marxian theory of value. I suggest that it can only lead to confusion in economic theory.

The same sort of reductive procedure is exhibited in Spencer's view of the place of science in education. Because of the undeniable fact that all educational materials can be considered scientifically, Spencer takes them all to be parts of science, and in such a way as to conceal their peculiar features even when some difference is verbally admitted. I should say that in general the opposition between a literary and a scientific education (using 'scientific' here to signify the operational outlook which is characteristic of the way science teaching has actually developed) is the opposition between a non-reductive and a reductive procedure, that is, between grasping qualitative distinctions and ignoring them or explaining them away.

That leads me to some further consideration of classicism. The importance of classics in education is that they are concerned with the permanent, not in Spencer's sense of the permanently useful but of what is independent of people's particular purposes at particular times, and therefore can carry over from one civilization to another. The position may be expressed roughly by saying that education is concerned to show the inferiority of the local and contemporary to the distant in space and time. This way of putting the matter may be exaggerated, but it is meant to be a strong expression of opposition to natural prejudice, namely, prejudice in favour of the local and contemporary, a prejudice which prevents the formation of objective standards of judgement.

The position, I think, is this. When we are concerned with the distant in either space or time, and especially in both, we are presented with material that has undergone a certain sifting. For example, while in the literature of contemporary France there may be just as much rubbish as in that of any contemporary English-speaking country, a good deal of this is sifted out, and what is transmitted to other countries is, in large measure, the more important. We cannot lay this down as an absolute rule, but there is a tendency in that direction. In passing between the two countries the material is subjected to a number of different criticisms. Even if there are some of the same weaknesses of judgement in both cultures, there are also differences in this respect, and so there tends to be a greater correction of faults in studying a foreign literature than in studying a local literature. Similarly, in studying the literature of our own country, we should in general find it more educative to go to the work of the past, that is, to material that has undergone sifting through many generations and has survived criticism from many different angles; though we still cannot lay it down absolutely that anything that appeals to many successive generations must be good.

It is not the case, then, that past judgement was better than present judgement, or that foreign judgement is better than local judgement, though both of these can in particular instances be the case and education should always keep these possibilities in mind. What is true is that in combining with present and local judgements some acquaintance with distant judgements, we get a better and more consistent standard, that is, a better sense of the ways in which works can be criticized. Thus the objection to the demand for 'the up-to-date' does not rest on any theory of progressive degeneration, though there may be good reason for regarding our own times as a period of degeneration, or on the arbitrary selection of a particular past time as giving the standard of judgement, but rather on the fact that, while we cannot in any case avoid the contemporary, since it is closely associated with our policies and preferences we can see it in better perspective if we have a wider acquaintance both with types of performance and with types of criticism.

If we are concerned with 'classics' in the ordinary sense, namely the productions of Graeco-Roman culture, then, *first*, the same general argument will apply, the argument from acquaintance with a variety of judgements. Here we should bear in mind the linguistic as well as the literary side of the matter, or the combination of the two, in so far as the very structure of a foreign language shows us different ways of attacking a subject from those we are accustomed to, those current in our society. Greek and Latin are important in having left a considerable deposit in our language, and especially in learned language, that is, the language not merely of science, but of law, politics, and social affairs generally. What is particularly important, in this connection, is the deposit they have left in thought, the fact that they provide the starting-point of critical thinking in most of the subjects of education.

That question of content as distinguished from structure or partly so, leads on to the *second* point, that there are some periods or states of civilization which are themselves more classical than others, that is, which are more marked by an objective treatment of things and are not dominated by petty interests.

Without adhering to simple optimism, without saying that what is good, meaning what is objective, in such productions of particular civilizations is bound to survive, while what is bad, in the sense of being subjective or appealing to narrow interests, is bound to perish, we can still recognize a tendency for the better, the more objective or universal, to persist: for the survival, in the process of 'sifting', of that which presents a more coherent position or gives a more settled standard of judgement. If we look at fifth and fourth century Athens, classical Athens, we see a great deal of provincialism and narrowness, something which would be true of any people of any period. However, we also see that our very knowledge of that provincialism depends on the preservation of the work of those who attack provincialism, especially the work of Plato, but also the work of the tragedians, dealing with the greater human issues and setting standards for subsequent drama and literature generally.

I should say that, in their greatest and most lasting works, the classical peoples, and especially the Greeks, exhibited an objective outlook, and left an important deposit of objectivism in our language and thinking; and, further, that defence of the classics turns on the contention that it is only by appreciating these works and what has flowed from them that we can get settled standards of aesthetic and thus of educated judgement. That is not to advocate mere appeal to the classical writers as authorities, the settling of a problem, for example, by quoting Plato. Plato himself would not have approved of that line. He was alive to the fact that we cannot solve problems by cut and dried formulae, but must have a critical attitude of mind working round any formula we use. This is also something which Arnold, with his training in Hellenism, specially emphasized. (In *Culture and Anarchy* Arnold compares Hellenism and Hebraism. Though he sees some good in Hebraism, in general he attacks it.) We can still learn positive lessons from Plato, especially on objectivity and judgement.

Now if we thus recognize *the* classical period, we can also recognize classical periods in the history and literature and general culture of other peoples, for example, the Elizabethan age in English culture, the eighteenth century in Scottish culture. That is why the study of the Elizabethan age, particularly, must form a part of any higher education in English culture, of any development for *us* of standards of judgement. Again, we might recognize a specially classical character in particular peoples, like the French. We might see that the French had been concerned in the preservation of certain elements of classical (Graeco-Roman) culture, and for that reason regard the French language and literature as having a special educational importance. Arnold does not bring out all these points quite explicitly, but that is the general direction of his argument.

When, on the other hand, we consider the attack of Spencer and others on classical education as being mainly of 'conventional value', we have to admit, *first*, that classics can be taught in a pedantic and routine way, just as science can, so that there is no such thing as a foolproof curriculum, and that there are other aspects of education than the curriculum. But the fact that teachers may not be alive to these other aspects is no argument against a given curriculum; and a pedantic or routine teaching of the classics is certainly not teaching in a classical or literary manner, not training in judgement.

Secondly, we must admit that people, when challenged, can give bad reasons for a quite good educational procedure. In fact, they will do so if they have not previously worked out an educational theory. First reactions to criticism are nearly always bad. But that does not prove that those who were subjected to this procedure are not educated. Spencer attacks some of these bad reasons, reasons stated in terms of *method* rather than *content*, such as that learning Latin and Greek is the best way of training the memory. He argues that science is just as good a way of training the memory, if not a better one, while it deals with more important material and thus gives a better educational foundation (Spencer, *Education*, especially pp. 44–5).

Dewey[4] handles the question of curriculum in a broader way than Spencer. He rejects the conception of training separate faculties, and particularly of doing so by means of separate subjects. He says quite rightly that this sort of argument is often of a manufactured character; that a person having a preference for or being accustomed to a particular arrangement and selection of studies looks for reasons why they should be included in an educational scheme and given a particular weight in that scheme, and finds the faculty explanation a convenient one.

Dewey quotes:

Memory is trained by most studies, but best by languages and history; taste is trained by the more advanced study of languages, and still better by English literature; imagination by all higher language teaching, but chiefly by Greek and Latin poetry; observation by science work in the laboratory, though some training is to be got from the earlier stages of Latin and Greek; for expression, Greek and Latin composition come first and English composition next; for abstract reasoning, mathematics stands almost alone; for concrete reasoning, science comes first, then geometry; for social reasoning, the Greek and Roman historians and orators come first, and general history next. Hence the narrowest education which can claim to be at all complete includes Latin, one modern language, some history, some English literature, and one science (pp. 285–6).

This example undoubtedly indicates that the person quoted has tried to work up reasons for what he prefers, but that would be nothing against the curriculum he actually does favour. Dewey, of course, is hostile to curricula schemes in general. He does not believe in the objectivity I have referred to, but in the development of a general 'human nature'. Thus,

[4] John Dewey, *Democracy and Education*, New York, 1916, Electrotyped Reprint 1948, Ch. 18.

he concentrates on *methods* and is critical of the emphasis on subjects, though in fact this leads him, as it leads most contemporary educationalists, to support utilitarian or practical subjects.

We find Dewey criticizing Spencer's view of the role of science in education not on the ground that science lacks the importance that Spencer attaches to it, but on the ground that he takes a wrong view of science itself. Spencer speaks of science as a body of truth, as a set of finished formulae. This is opposed to what Dewey regards as the most important function of science in education: that it encourages the student to wrestle with problems, that it introduces him to methods of working on material and not just to a body of results. (In so far as science is reductive, it would lead to concentration on results, and much science teaching is of that kind.)

Now, what Dewey may be said to be opposing here is the mere exercise of authority, the teacher's simply laying down the law to the pupil. Allowing some force to that criticism, we must observe that Spencer specifically says that scientific training is superior to linguistic training in being less authoritative, in that pupils do not simply have to be told something, say that 'logos' means discourse, but can see the connections for themselves or can see how the propositions of science hold. Spencer admits, of course, that there are some real connections on the linguistic side, so that some account can be given of why this means that, but he maintains that such connections cannot at all be understood by beginners, who have simply to accept the fact that a certain word has a certain meaning or that a certain construction is grammatically correct (Spencer, *Education*, p. 46).

It should be noted here that there is a definite limit to the finding of reasons even in science, to seeing how it is that something is the case. In any given instance our argument must start from certain premises which we simply take to be true. While, in the teaching of science, it is possible, though by no means regularly the case, that the pupils themselves see these things to be so, we have to remember that, on the language side, to observe something to be so is to observe a specific use of language, and that the discourse of the teacher is, to a large extent, the actual use of language which the pupils have to observe. Naturally the teacher's discourse represents a broader use of language with which the children are not in contact, or not in so thorough a way, but the same would apply to the teaching of science: here we find a certain restricted and selected presentation from material which extends beyond the course of training.

The question of the teacher's authority, then, is not so simple as it appears at first sight and as it appears to Spencer. But, further, we may consider here Arnold's insistence on the need for authority, for what he calls recognition of the findings of 'right reason' as opposed to simply doing what we like. Arnold's position was apparently influenced by idealist theories similar to those of T. H. Green. We might have doubts about the doctrine of a 'best self' which can be brought out in everyone, and equally about the doctrine of a community or reconcilability of all such best selves, but we must certainly agree that there can be no education on the principle that one opinion is as good as another. That principle leads to mere acquiescence in the existence of a multiplicity of views so far as these can exist together or, so far as they cannot, to suppression of one view by another. There can be no education where truth is decided by voting or by fighting; and Arnold's support of 'right reason' here can be connected with his position in *Literature and Dogma*, that there are certain standards of judgement, and that there is a training in judgement even if its findings are often tentative, are not fixed formulae.

Thus, without setting up a doctrine of political authority we could still speak of the judgements of those who followed a particular tradition as having authority, as having a certain weight as compared with the judgements of the first-comer, of someone entering the field for the first time. The authority of good judgement would not, of course, amount to much unless the upholders of the tradition in question had a certain political force, a certain power of influencing events; and that means unless they had some kind of organization, that is, unless there were what I call 'colleges' or 'schools' which are the bearers of cultural traditions. Though, again, to have an influence such schools must have a flexible policy, that is, ways of impressing their views on people outside the tradition or not so thoroughly immersed in it, since, otherwise, if it came to a simple question of force the bearers of such traditions would always be defeated.

It might be said that a community is in a high state of culture when such colleges are recognized, when it is widely acknowledged that the bearers of certain traditions are in some sense authorities in their fields, when some deference is paid to their views both in their special line and in regard to the place of their special interest in general social life. The continuance of such traditions calls for the exercise of that judgement of which Arnold speaks, and is opposed to the supremacy of science, at least in Spencer's sense as a body of definite truth. The point is that science, including physical science, develops in terms of social interests: it develops as a means of facilitating the particular operations which have the most powerful backing in a given state of society.

I have argued that, as it appears in education, what science amounts to is the learning of a set of devices which facilitate particular operations, namely those which happen to be socially important at the time, and that criticism will only come by emphasis on the other side, the linguistic or literary side. That is not to say that science, as science, would not be better if a criticism of conceptions were carried on concurrently with the discovery of propositions or the learning of procedures, but I think it is still the case, even apart from the special history of science, that this critical outlook could never be arrived at on the side of science alone, and that it does require those literary and cultural studies which are contrasted with scientific study as it actually exists. Spencer's procedure, then, in subordinating those other studies to the study of science or postponing them, ensures an illiberal treatment of the questions; it ensures that reductive procedure of which I spoke, and the absence of a criticism of categories and conceptions.

This reductive tendency appears also in Spencer's substantially reducing human science to physical science. He assumes, in particular, that physical science gives us a policy in human affairs. Spencer reveals the weakness of his position especially in his doctrine of the 'unknowable', of what he calls 'the Ultimate Cause of things which science cannot enable us to comprehend'. Science, he says, leads us everywhere 'to boundaries that we cannot cross' (Spencer, *Education*, p. 49). It is worth observing that, even if however much we know there is always something we do not know, this does not mean that there are any fixed or final boundaries of our knowledge. But, in any case, that is a philosophical point, and Spencer's doctrine of the unknowable comes to this, that science cannot solve philosophical problems; though it might equally be said that there are *scientific* problems that a reductive science cannot solve. There are always things that are inexplicable in terms of our 'units' or 'elements', whatever these might happen to be. The remedy is to be philosophical or critical from the beginning, and this means bringing science down from the place assigned to it by Spencer in the training of the mind.

IV. Education as Classical and as Training of Judgement

Arnold, in various of his writings, attacks the narrow and practical conception of education that is upheld by people like Spencer. What he particularly opposes is the abandonment of traditions, the assumption that we can 'start from scratch', that we can deal with educational matters by the 'light of reason' or by considering at large whether this or that is desirable without reference to models or established standards, taking these, in fact, simply as an impediment to education. This procedure leads in general to a loss of understanding, and in particular to what Arnold calls the 'degeneration of style'. This is something which is especially marked in the degradation of language, which is taken merely as an instrument, that is, as subordinate to the advancement of the particular things which its users are aiming at. Since these users have little or no contact with the traditions embedded in language and literature, there is a loss of exactness of expression. Something is used which is 'good enough' for the purpose, and refinements of meaning simply disappear. At present we find this exemplified in the utterances of people who speak in the name of education but who are interested in 'reform' or 'social improvement'. We find in them the degenerate style and degraded use of language which Arnold refers to and, of course, as professional educators they are able to accelerate the degradation.

Arnold emphasizes this sort of point in the article called 'The Function of Criticism at the Present Time'; the point, namely, that this degradation is bound up with the advancing of particular aims, the desire to carry out certain policies, to make what are deemed to be 'social improvements'. As he puts it, 'the mass of mankind will never have any ardent zeal for seeing things as they are; very inadequate ideas will always satisfy them'.[5] That indicates the weakness of the supporters of a universal education, an education for the masses, as against an education which is directed to seeing things as they are. The sort of information which is wanted by the people Arnold is criticizing is that which serves some practical purpose, and when they have arrived at ideas which serve their purposes the devotees of a special interest suspend their criticism or inquiry. It is here that we find the flourishing of the 'good enough' or 'just as good' which, as I suggested, is a symptom of degenera-

[5] Arnold, *Essays in Criticism*, 1891 ed., p. 25.

tion, that is, the degeneration of thinking or of seeing things as they are. Thus, Arnold attacks the view that we can simply reject tradition, start again at any given point and get a satisfactory arrangement of things; that we can invent the whole thing for ourselves as we go along and remodel all institutions according to first principles, that is, in terms of a general notion of desirability and without reference to history.

To sum up: the turning of education to practical ends means the limitation of inquiry in accordance with these ends; and the inadequacy of current doctrines of reform lies in the fact that they are uncritical or take certain social ends for granted. Criticism, according to Arnold, is *a disinterested endeavour to learn and propagate the best that is known and thought in the world'* (p. 138). Here he emphasizes the importance of foreign literature, and the weakness of the view that regards only the local product as good, and either does not subject it to the standards that would be applied to literature in general, or takes it as itself the standard. The view maintained in England that English literature is outstanding, even if it could have some argumentative support from those who had considered the bulk of the relevant material, would appeal to and be echoed by those who had not made the necessary comparisons and indeed were not in a position to do so; and it would be one of the factors preventing them from extending their knowledge of literature, from becoming more critical or having more exact standards.

Arnold's position suggests that education cannot be a universal thing, that we cannot have education for everybody, though we might have a certain participation in education (an approach to judgement) on the part of people who do not go the whole way, that is, do not become thoroughly critically minded. If we use the special term 'scholarship', it could be argued that it was favourable to the flourishing of scholarship in a community if people who did not become scholars at least went far enough to have an appreciation of scholarship. In that case scholarship would have a certain social standing and would not be confined to a few struggling against the social stream, though I should say that there would always be something of this character, something of a struggle against commercial or other narrow interests in the existence of scholarship anywhere. Even so, we have fluctuation in the social strength of education in this sense, or in the sense of judgement; and Arnold contends that the English literature of his period (mid-nineteenth century and a little later) does not stand up to the test at all well, the test, namely, of the best that is known and thought on any subject; though, apart from that existing situation, he attacks national separatism in general, and insists that English literature (or culture) should be treated as a part of European literature (or culture).

Summing up, then, we either have an education which is 'universal' in the sense of developing general standards of judgement but is not 'universal' in the sense of being for everyone; or else we have a general education in which standards are lost, that is, in which what are set up as standards are dictated by practical and local considerations, and with this goes the doctrine I mentioned of the 'just as good' in the use of language or in thinking generally, which, whether or not it is a cause, is certainly a symptom of cultural degeneration. I should argue that utilitarianism is one of the outlooks preparing the way for such degeneration.

I have suggested that education as the development of judgement or of criticism is the development of an objective view of things, which again I have described as the classical view. I should say that, *firstly*, a training in judgement involves training in logic, which we might roughly describe as the theory of the conditions of existence or of the characters of things as real. Training in logic gives us standards of judgement whereby we can recognize fallacy, which can be described as believing that a relation of implication exists where in fact it does not. Such logical criticism would not be possible unless we recognized implication and also non-implication as real relations existing within any material, as contrasted with the view that the rules of logic are something imposed upon the material, for example by our thinking. The latter view could only mean that our thinking was unsound, and that we did not have general standards of criticism. Similarly, we should have standards derived from the theory of definition and classification or, again, from the theory of causality. If we regard causality as a feature of existence as such, then on that view of the objective facts we should reject as illogical any indeterminist theory. Broadly, then, from logic as a general theory of existence we get logic in a more special sense, as a set of criteria applicable to any material.

The second requirement for judgement or criticism depends on a point already made, namely, that it is not in general possible to find fallacies in reasoning on any subject by a knowledge of logic alone. We need knowledge of the subject too, and we cannot derive a position on a subject simply from logic. Again, our study of logic is bound up with our human associations; it takes place not in a vacuum but by our entering into some movement of thought. In fact, we approach logical questions not by a bare study of the facts but by considering human procedures in relation to the facts, that is, the sort of things that human beings say or mean, and the sort of confusions and errors that they fall into. Even the notion of fallacy is not a part of objective logic. What we find there is the notion of non-implication, apart from the question whether any particular person would take it to be implication. But even beyond the question of formal fallacy, the recognition of which does not depend on a special knowledge of humanity, we have what is called 'material fallacy'. This is something that can never be fully dealt with by logicians, though many of them make some attempt at it, because it is concerned with the kinds of error to which human beings are prone, and any thorough consideration of it would involve reference to both psychological and social material. I should take, then, as the *second* main requirement for judgement or criticism, an understanding of the main types of human confusion and illusion or of the kinds and conditions of human error, of the tendencies in human nature that lead to a neglect or distortion of logic.

Thirdly, I should say that judgement requires a knowledge of what is permanent in human affairs, that is, a knowledge of the major departments of human achievement, such as science, art, and industry, which I take to constitute culture and to be the real subject-matter of ethics. Here again it is vital to see that understanding of culture cannot be deduced from logic alone: while the logician often seems to be expert in a field of which he knows little, because he can point out fallacies, his criticism will not go very far without special knowledge of the field, enabling him to know, for example, what are the omitted premises in a given argument. A person who tries to settle all questions on the basis of logic alone is really deficient in judgement, and his logic soon turns into sophistry or eristic. An outstanding example of this is given in Plato's *Euthydemus*, where we have sophists who, by a few argumentative devices, profess to settle any question, or at least refute any other person's theory in any field.

The *fourth* requirement for judgement is, over and above a knowledge of what is permanent, a knowledge of what is timely, that is, of what are the issues of the moment, what are the main present obstacles to understanding and the main present opportunities for understanding. While the first three requirements help to determine the fourth, they do not determine it entirely. While this element in judgement is perhaps the hardest to describe, we might refer to it as a historical sense, a sense of the development and changes of things, additional to the sense of continuance. The relation between the knowledge of past history and judgement of present issues is one of mutual assistance; that is, our interest in current issues and our interest in past events reinforce one another or strengthen our understanding in both fields.

The four elements in judgement recognized in this rather

rough account may be referred to as the 'logical', 'psychological', 'cultural' and 'historical'. They are all necessary to the
educated man, and they cannot be amalgamated or reduced to
one. To try to do so would only lead to confusion and looseness of thought. Such looseness is exhibited in Dewey's use of
the vague term 'significance' in order to show the place of
some particular type of development in what he regards as
education.

V. Education and 'Progress'

Dewey says that 'a community or social group maintains itself
through continuous self-renewal' and that 'this renewal takes
place by means of the educational growth of the immature
members of the group'. The question here is of social continuity or the maintaining of certain characters of a given
society; and for this it is seen to be necessary that successive
generations should ripen, or that the immature should become
mature. This is similar to the conception we found in Spencer
of education as covering all acquisitions, everything that the
child comes to be able to do which he was not initially able to
do.

As far as this description goes, we do not find in it the
conception of 'progress' which commonly appears in educational theory and, indeed, in Dewey's own later discussion. As
far as the question of renewal is concerned, we might take
Dewey here to be alive to the point that the pupil's progressing
or making a series of acquisitions does not imply that the
society progresses, but would be necessary for the society
merely to maintain itself. But, even in this initial formula, he is
at least making another assumption, the assumption of what I
call 'solidarism' or 'social unity', because the question posed is
that of the continuance of the social group as a unit; and not of
a variety of types of social activity in competition with one
another, where the conditions of the continuance, and again of

the extension of one such activity, are quite different from the conditions of the continuance or extension of another.

This is a point of great educational importance. If we make the main question that of the survival of society in general, then we are denying the conflict between the interest in learning and other interests. We are especially ignoring the fact that even what are called 'educational institutions' are of a compromise character; and that, instead of having a single object, they are adjustments among competing interests, each of which does as well as it can under the circumstances. We are, then, ignoring the view which, associating the name 'education' especially with some or one of these interests, regards the operation of others as miseducation, that is, as repressing rather than developing the capacity for learning.

This assumption of unity is connected again with the type of view that I call 'voluntarism'. This is the view that the question simply is of getting a policy and putting it into effect, so that people ask what single thing shall we devote our educational institutions to: Shall it be learning? vocation? social service? I should say that the proper question for a person interested in learning as a social phenomenon is: How does the interest in learning maintain itself in institutions of such a mixed character, or in the field of struggling social tendencies generally; or to what extent does learning flourish in such and such institutions? These are questions which do not of themselves suggest that the interest in learning either could absorb the whole institution or be squeezed out of it altogether.

In his later argument Dewey at least implies that there are such varying and conflicting interests, though he never emphasizes or fully develops the point. He also agrees that the school is not the sole organ of training for the young, though he is working towards a position in which it would become increasingly so. (This is largely the position of our modern educators, influenced by Dewey.) He also agrees that the school is not the sole condition, though it is one of the conditions, of the continuance of society or of a particular kind of society. But his treatment of diversity is very loose. He admits that a modern society is many societies more or less loosely connected, but he goes on to say that, as a society becomes more enlightened, it realizes that it is responsible not for transmitting and conserving the whole of its existing achievements but only such as make for a 'better' future society. He adds that the school is society's chief agency for the accomplishment of this end.

That means that Dewey is now introducing the conception of 'progress' as against mere continuance. He is assuming a progressive reduction of social diversity, or diversity of interests. Even now he is clinging sufficiently to the conception of social unity to say that it is society that has the function of continuing the better and weeding out the inferior, whereas clearly he ought to say that certain social interests, by means of an educational or some other mechanism, are able to abolish certain other social interests. In other words, while verbally admitting diversity, he wants also to hold to unity; and, while beginning with the question of continuance, he goes over to the question of progress, but leaves it entirely vague, *firstly*, just what 'being better' involves or what precise description of 'improvement' we could give, and, *secondly*, what section of society is enforcing what it considers to be improvements and weeding out other sections.

What I suggested as a criterion of education, namely judgement, is of a fairly general character, but I still say that we can distinguish between the sort of training that develops judgement and the sort that destroys or discourages judgement. Putting it in other terms, we can distinguish between the advancement of learning and the obstruction of learning; and in such terms as these we might be able to decide whether a society or an educational system was undergoing improvement. But if we simply say that it is the business of the responsible citizen in general, or the educator in particular, to 'improve' things, to make them 'better', then we are not conveying any positive position, and we are ignoring conflicts—conflicts, among other things, about what does and does not constitute improvement.

We could formulate this *first* criticism, in a crude way, by asking who it is that decides what is and what is not improvement, by pointing to the vagueness of the notion of improvement itself, and by suggesting that we are being asked quite arbitrarily to take it that some forces and not others are on the side of improvement. This means that we are being asked to accept an ethical position, or a position with ethical aspects, without any direct discussion of ethical questions. This is clearly true of Spencer, but theories of education generally assume some ethic without working it out to show its soundness.

Passing on to the *second* criticism I made of Dewey, that he leaves it vague what section of society is enforcing 'improvements', we find that Dewey simply assumes that the educators will be of a certain type and that the persons in charge of education will be those devoted to the same values. Here we could criticize Dewey in two ways: namely, in his assuming that he knows, and his readers will agree, that certain values are sound and that people who take the same view as his are in charge of education.

If, on the other hand, we take a positive view, if we even appeal to something so general as the formation of judgement, then we are in a position to say not only that there are forces supporting this and forces opposing it in society, but that there are such forces in the educational systems themselves. Further, we can now claim, with justification, that discussion of education as it occurs in society and in these institutions requires a positive treatment of the actual clash between such forces, as distinct from vague talk about a 'social function' of education and what education could do in the way of 'improvement' if it were wholly devoted to improvement. If we take a positive view, a view which we have seen will involve disputes about subject-matter, that is, about what is educationally central (as in the 'classical versus scientific' controversy), then we shall have to take education as flourishing in some societies or in some periods and languishing in others, though even when it flourishes most it will have serious obstacles to face. But even if a society were degenerating, so that judgement is becoming weaker in it, that would not affect the character of education in so far as it does persist. It would not alter the fact that becoming educated involves gaining contact with certain traditions or movements of thought. Indeed, it would only be by making such contacts that a person could even learn that such degeneration was taking place. If Dewey, for example, were to say that the doctrine of judgement is arbitrary, it could be answered that he at least has no criterion at all when he appeals to a notion of 'betterment' that everyone is supposed to be able to accept.

Dewey's attitude also exhibits what may be called his 'practicalism'. No doubt we should have to agree that he is supporting certain kinds of practice against others, but he still takes being or not being practical as a criterion for determining what is and what is not to be admitted to an educational scheme; and in chapter six he uses the criterion of practicality in opposition to a certain feature of education which he calls 'classical' when he says:

'The study of past *products* will not help us to understand the present, because the present is not due to the products, but to the life of which they were the products. A knowledge of the past and its heritage is of great significance when it enters into the present, but not otherwise. And the mistake of making the records and remains of the past the main material of education is that it cuts the vital connection of present and past, and tends to make the past a rival of the present and the present a more or less futile imitation of the past. Under such circumstances, culture becomes an ornament and solace; a refuge and an asylum.' (Dewey, *Democracy and Education*, p. 88.)

We do, of course, live in the present; but we are still living in the present when we examine and appreciate the products of the past, even if we stop at appreciation and do not make it subserve further activities. Dewey is simply assuming here that certain forms of practice and procedure are 'vital' and others are not, just as he assumes that culture cannot be the possession of a few but must be distributed widely. His argument loses its force if these assumptions are not made. We can also question his distinction between study of the products and study of the life which produced them. It is only by studying the products of past cultures that we can study the cultural activity involved; and, admitting that such products can be studied pedantically, as the mere grammarian studies the Greek and Latin classics, we have to recognize that a contemporary culture can equally be dealt with pedantically, that is, by reference to its externals and not to its actual movements.

It is false, then, that a man is not living in the present when he appreciates a Platonic dialogue or a play of Sophocles, and it is absurd to say that a work is not really 'living' unless it produces some roughly conceived betterment for people in general. But it has still to be remembered that these classical products do not come to us in isolation but in connection with what has been a continuous tradition, a tradition of active study and positive standards. Even if a person steeped in such traditions is unable to act effectively in current affairs, he may still be able to judge them better than those in control of them; and his educated judgement will, I suggest, involve a rejection of the ideology of betterment, however prevalent that may be.

Dewey passes on from this vague notion of betterment, and the assumption of control by those devoted to betterment, to the question of democracy in education (chapter seven); and he speaks of the need for a measure of the worth of any given mode of social life. Arnold's view, it will be remembered, is that we improve our powers of criticism by getting acquainted with the best that has been thought and known on various subjects and by developing a play of the mind around these subjects, or by becoming absorbed in certain movements. As against Arnold, Dewey appears to be looking for some simple criterion, some set of fixed formulae, and to this extent he seems to be going back on his criticism of Spencer's notion of science as the criterion of worth.

The criterion of the worth of any mode of social life Dewey finds in 'cooperation'. He points out, as Socrates does in the *Republic*, Book I, that even in a gang of thieves there must be some common interest and cooperative activity; but, firstly, the types of cooperation are limited, since the interests shared by the thieves lack variety, and, secondly, there is a lack of cooperation between this group and other groups. That illustrates Dewey's criterion of the best education, an education that in particular is democratic: an educational system should embrace the maximum number of common interests and should have the maximum amount of communication with other forms of social life, with 'society in general'.

Now, as I have already suggested, the educated man is one who has a certain contact with, and a certain power of judging, a large number of subjects and activities, if only in so far as he has a command of logic. But that still does not amount to participation in those activities and, considering the matter the other way round, participation in all or many of those activities does not give one a command of logic or standards of judgement.

Referring back to the *Republic*, we may notice that the Socratic ethic is a formal one. It uses the formal criterion of cooperation or agreement, and not the positive or concrete criterion of some specific quality. This at least appears to save trouble: it is easier to detect cooperation than to detect a positive quality, and we can get a quite general admission that certain groups are cooperating, though there might be a dispute as to the depth or thoroughness of the cooperation. But in the case of a quality, goodness, if we find that some recognize it and others do not, there seems to be no way of settling the argument.

However, once anyone admits, as Socrates had to do, that

there is never perfect harmony or cooperation in human affairs, then he will have the greatest difficulty in deciding along what line an increase of harmony is to be sought. (This is similar to the difficulty, when 'consistency' is taken to be the criterion of truth, of deciding which of two incompatible theories is to be abandoned.) In fact, disagreement in practical life consists in devotion to qualitatively different things, and the criterion of agreement does not apply; that is, disagreement is not a reason for anyone's giving up his specific attachment in favour of anyone else's. The view may be taken, and this is my own view, that good activities do cooperate or communicate with one another, but that has to be found out after we can recognize the good activities themselves. It cannot be used as a means of recognizing goodness. For one thing, goodness does not cooperate with everything; it opposes evils, even though it might employ different methods in its opposition from those which evils employ in opposition to it.

We cannot, then, take cooperation, communication or agreement as our criterion of educational worth. If we have a qualitative criterion, even though this makes our position more difficult in some respects, then we have to accept the fact of struggle or opposition and cannot take comprehensiveness or all-inclusiveness as our ideal. We should rather have to say that learning occupies a special and precarious position among other interests, so that we cannot even expect to have a general educational system in which education prevails, but rather it will be one ingredient or force within such a system. We have to conclude, then, that Dewey's democratic criterion, in the sense of embracing everything in education, is opposed to the spirit of learning. We might agree that other interests in the same institutions have to draw upon learning to some extent, and that this is why they go on together, even if not in thorough agreement. But that does not imply that we could ever have a unitedly functioning system in which learning has its definite place. What we rather have is a struggle in which, at times, learning advances and, at other times, regresses.

One important point here (that is, apart from what I take to be the falsity of Dewey's criterion of complete communication or equality, the breaking down of all barriers) is that the very fact of aiming at such an objective may be prejudicial (I should say, is prejudicial) to special qualitative activities that find it possible to exist under conditions of inequality. In practice egalitarian policies have had the effect of weakening learning or criticism. The egalitarian policy is defended by the argument that if in a life of the quality X you have broad communication (what Dewey calls 'a sharing of many and varied interests'), then you can maintain X simply by aiming at communication or the breaking down of barriers. This argument is simply fallacious. A question that arises here is how far democracy in an egalitarian sense (the breaking down of divisions) is to be identified with, or is even compatible with liberty. What has to be considered is whether liberty does not exist in the struggle of diverse interests or in the character of certain of the struggling forces and not in the system as a whole, so that the policy of reducing diversity is actually inimical to liberty.

Dewey seems to fall into contradiction on these matters. He wishes to have an all-inclusive education; and he takes this to imply, among other things, that regard will be paid to the uniqueness of every individuality, so that 'education' will mean something different for every different pupil. Previously, however, he had contrasted the education that aims merely at perpetuating customs and established social differences with that in which the best customs and interests will be selected and developed and the worst will be eliminated. To say that we encourage in every pupil what we judge to be best does not really square with saying that we are encouraging special aptitudes or having regard to the fitness of every individual. In fact, the latter conception might be taken to imply a separate school for every person. Again, having spoken of this infinite variability, Dewey goes on to say, and indeed to represent as the other side of the same fact, that 'in the degree in which society has become democratic, social organization means utilization of the specific and variable qualities of individuals, not stratification by classes'. The word 'utilization' here would seem to imply some agency which fits all the individual talents into a general scheme, that is, which treats them as means; and this is in line with Dewey's previous conception of a total system directed by people with a particular view of what is better, even though he also calls this 'direction by society'.

In order to get out of these difficulties we have to do two things: *first*, to see 'education' as having a constant meaning and not as varying from individual to individual; and, *second*, to reject the view of education as a vehicle for social change, the means by which society reorganizes itself. Once more, if we take this view in opposition to Dewey we see education, in the strict sense, as only one struggling tendency, not merely in society but in the institutions that are called 'educational'.

In line with his 'democratic' conception of education, Dewey attacks Plato (that is, Socrates in the *Republic*) for lumping people into a few sharply divided classes instead of taking account of individuality. But he does not show how a scheme to provide something special for every individual is possible; and he ignores the fact that Socrates is concerned here with those differences that are politically important, and is not excluding variety of development within each class. For example, a large number of different aptitudes will be developed within the industrial class, for which, in any case, Socrates has not worked out a scheme of education.

Further, we can criticize the notion which Dewey finds in eighteenth century individualism, a position which he criticizes only on the organizational side, of a complete and harmonious development of all powers, which moreover is taken to be harmonious with the aims of humanity as a whole. We can say, *first*, as we said of Socrates in the *Republic*, that it is a mere assumption that the developments of all personalities must harmonize with one another. In fact, it is actually opposed to our experience. *Secondly*, we can reject both the notion of the 'full development of personality' and that of 'the aims of humanity as a whole'. We have to recognize, in the latter case, that there are always opposing aims; and, in the former, that there are inconsistent possibilities of development, so that when a person develops in one way, that prevents his developing in another way which, to begin with, was equally possible.

Dewey refers here to Kant's view that all culture begins with private men and spreads outward from them, and that rulers are simply interested in such training as will make their subjects better tools for their own intentions. Kant's view, while it is expressed in a rather individualistic way, is sounder than Dewey's, in recognizing that the acquisition of learning is a special kind of thing, that the question of education is quite different from that of complete social organization, and that attempts at complete social organization conflict with education.

When Dewey says, 'The conception of education as a social process and function has no definite meaning until we define the kind of society we have in mind' (*Democracy and Education*, p. 112) he is assuming that society works as a totality which has its appropriate educational aspect (totalitarian education for a totalitarian society, democratic education for a democratic society, and so on), instead of seeing education as a distinct kind of thing that occurs in all kinds of society, although it is variously affected, helped and hindered, by surrounding social conditions. Again, when Dewey admits, as he does in effect, that we simply have to make up our minds, without any possibility of conclusive argument, whether we prefer democracy or non-democracy and that we will then have a notion of education that fits in with that preference, he is still implying that education as such has no definite character. On the other hand, Dewey does try to insinuate certain arguments for democracy. He uses the notion of cooperation or communication as his criterion both of what is a good society and of what is truly education. At the same time, while he professes to be democratic he is dubiously so. He speaks of the 'freeing of individual capacity in a progressive growth directed to social ends' (p. 115), which reminds us of Rousseau's conception of forcing people to be free.

Either, then, we have to use the word 'education' in the vague sense of training for any purpose whatever, which would cut across Dewey's suggested criterion of 'cooperation'; or we have to use it as referring to a specific kind of training, say intellectual training, and in that case the question of its occurrence is quite distinct from the character of the society within which it occurs. There would be societies which are more opposed than others to education in this sense, but the criterion of the occurrence of education would not be such features as social harmony but just the character of education itself.

VI. 'Aims' of Education

Dewey discusses the aims of education in chapters eight and nine of *Democracy and Education*. The general position I have been putting forward would lead us to say that what we have to discuss is the character of education and not a set of aims, least of all a policy for society in general or a recipe for social improvement. We could call education 'progressive' in the sense that so far as people are educated they become more critical, but that implies nothing as to what might be called 'general social advancement'.

Now Dewey has certain criticisms to offer of the notion of aims in education, but these criticisms are not very effective. We find him once more, in concluding this part of the discussion, talking quite specifically of aims, of what should be the aim of education in our time. First, he attacks the notion of an aim as something imposed on education from without. He thinks education is distorted by such imposition and that the aim should be taken as a result arising from the process of education itself. As he puts it: 'An aim denotes the result of any natural process brought to consciousness and made a factor in determining present observation and choice of ways of acting. It signifies that an activity has become intelligent.' (p. 129). So he thinks that the nature and the range of the aims of any process become more definite as the activity proceeds, as against the notion of fixed aims with which we enter upon the activity and which we continue to pursue after we engage in it. Here Dewey treats the conception of means and end as relatively unimportant. It is a question, he hints, of successive stages in a continuous development.

We might agree with the rejection of imposed aims, and still not think that the progressive formulation of aims had the importance that Dewey attaches to it, in particular not regard it as a mark of intelligence. Intelligence, we might say, is directed on the subject-matter, the material we are dealing with, rather than on the activity itself. Intelligence involves making distinctions and finding connections, but does not necessarily or usually involve framing a policy. If we were thinking of the working of (mental) interests themselves, and not of specific things aimed at, we should have to shift the emphasis from procedure to subject-matter and to take a less 'practical' line than Dewey does.

Even in agreeing with Dewey's opposition to policies imposed from outside we have to consider exactly what they are imposed on, just what sort of activities may be distorted to serve an external purpose. Here Dewey takes a quite individualistic line. He makes it a question of imposition on individual pupils, though he has the same difficulties as before in reconciling the development of personality and the general betterment or advance to higher social levels which he takes to be characteristic of education. Thus he says:

And it is well to remind ourselves that education as such has no aims. Only persons, parents, and teachers, etc., have aims, not an abstract idea like education. And consequently their purposes are indefinitely varied, differing with different children, changing as children grow and with the growth of experience on the part of the one who teaches. Even the most valid aims which can be put in words will, as words, do more harm than good unless one recognizes that they are not aims, but rather suggestions to educators as to how to observe, how to look ahead, and how to choose in liberating and directing the energies of the concrete situations in which they find themselves. (p. 125).

Here Dewey has a confused notion of 'aim' and his reasons for saying education has no aim are not sound. On the sort of view he has, the view, namely, that there is any number of purposes operating in education, education can only mean training, that is, the condition of acquiring some characteristic or some mode of activity not previously possessed, no matter what that might be. From that point of view there would be no specially educational institutions; education would be exhibited in the greatest variety of institutions, in the whole of society we might say.

Now, Dewey cannot consistently adhere to this exceedingly vague view, even though the criterion he suggests at the end of the passage quoted, namely 'liberating', is still rather indefinite, all the more so when he combines it with 'directing'. He is faced, then, with the dilemma either to use 'education' in such a broad sense that it will be impossible to speak of special educational institutions, or to recognize that education is something specific, that is, to recognize what later on he calls in question, namely, general ends in education or general characters of education. This generality does not make education more abstract or remote, but makes it more concrete, because it involves saying that education is a certain kind of acquisition and not just acquisition in general. So, if there is some criterion for distinguishing education from just any sort of training, then the notion of imposition from outside should be understood as imposition upon the educational sort of activity, not as imposition upon an individual, a person; for, while a person could not begin to be educated unless he had some initial aptitude when he did come into educational institutions and was subjected to certain pressures, it is still a particular interest that is developed in education, and not just any interest that any pupil happens to have. Thus, Dewey's rejection of imposition from without is actually misleading: it actually confuses the question what it is that may or may not be subjected to outside control.

I have also argued, of course, that educational activity as such does not operate freely even in what are called 'educational' institutions, that it is subject to hindrance and opposition there. But that reinforces the point that we cannot get a formula for satisfying its requirements along with those of every other type of activity in those institutions; that is, we cannot get what Dewey considers to be a democratic formula for education.

Dewey employs various devices for concealing the opposition here referred to. One of them is the use of the expression 'significance'. He says, for example: 'Until the democratic criterion of the intrinsic significance of every growing experience is recognized, we shall be intellectually confused by the demand for adaptation to external aims' (p. 127) and 'how can there be a society really worth serving unless it is constituted of individuals of significant personal qualities?' (p. 142). I take it that in the main Dewey uses the expressions 'significant' and 'significance' to avoid saying 'valuable' and 'value', that is, to suggest that he is giving a description and not just making a demand. But I also think he uses these expressions to suggest that there is something of the special educational character in anything at all that can be called 'individual development' or a 'growing experience'.

In chapter nine we find Dewey discussing, with reference to Rousseau, the conception of 'natural development' as the aim of education. Dewey considers that there are weaknesses in this conception, especially as Rousseau handles it, but also in the alternative conception of 'social efficiency' as the aim of education. But his criticism, in the end, amounts to this: that these two aims ought to be combined, and he assumes that it is possible to combine them.

Dewey thinks that Rousseau is concerned in the first instance with what might be called a 'natural physical aim', namely, health, and Dewey is prepared to concede that there is this natural physical aim, but he denies that it has the primary place that Rousseau allots to it. But if we are going to talk about a natural physical aim we could equally talk about a natural mental aim, what might roughly be called the possession of one's intellectual powers or competence, or again, along the special line that I have been arguing, one's competence in criticism. This would be an ability to deal with intellectual situations in general, just as health could be described as an ability to deal with physical situations.

That raises the question I have frequently mentioned, namely, whether there is a universal aptitude for criticism, that is, whether criticism is really embraced by the so-called 'democratic' view. The important point, however, is the inconsistency of such aims: the fact that aiming at health can in many ways cut across aiming at criticism or, more broadly, the fact that there is no systematic unity of what may be called natural aims, so that if we are to have a definite view of education we must connect it with some aims and not others. That is, we have to treat education as quite independent of those other aims.

Admittedly Dewey's democratic view of education purports to overcome such objections. He would say that there can be provision among the multitude of aims of an educational institution for a particular aim, such as the development of criticism; that is, even if we do not take education to be development of scholarship, still, according to Dewey, there would be room for the training of scholars in what is called the democratic educational system. But I should argue that this is not so: that the other forms of training would interfere with training in scholarship, and that we do find such interference; but that, in fact, it helps to maintain the scholarly position if someone has a clear academic view and brings out the untenability of Dewey's conception of an aim which embraces all particular aims.

We have an exhibition of Dewey's lack of an academic view and of what I should call his 'philistinism' in the following passage: 'There is nothing peculiar about educational aims. They are just like aims in any directed occupation. The educator, like the farmer, has certain things to do, certain resources with which to do, and certain obstacles with which to contend' (p. 124). Alternatively, we can take this to illustrate Dewey's utilitarianism, that is, as indicating the domination of his thinking, in spite of occasional waverings, by the conception of means and end, and his failure to recognize a certain character of mind or a certain way of life to which I have been referring by means of terms like 'scholarly' and 'critical'.

Summing up his whole argument on aims—trying to bring together natural development and social efficiency, and contradicting his previous assertion that education has no aims—Dewey has the following remarks to make on what he calls 'the dualism of self-development and service'. This dualism, he says, 'is too deeply established to be easily overthrown; for that reason, it is the particular task of education at the present time to struggle in behalf of an aim in which social efficiency and personal culture are synonymous instead of antagonists'. (p. 144).

We notice, firstly, that education, the abstract entity which Dewey said could not have aims, is here said to have a particular task and to struggle in behalf of a certain aim. But the main point is this contention that 'social efficiency' and 'personal culture' are to become synonymous instead of antagonists. This is the assumption of voluntarism, the assumption that if you want something it can be done, or if you want two things they cannot be incompatible. In the same question-begging way, 'liberation' and 'direction' can become synonymous, or force can be identified with freedom. Dewey's assumption is that if the claim of self-development and the claims of social service are opposed in any given situation, this must be regarded as an accident, something not inherent in the facts but due to a wrong way of looking at the facts.

This assumption is similar to the one I have attributed to the utilitarians, and especially to Owen, that if there are any disputes among people, they are due just to lack of information, and if all parties had the right information they would inevitably agree. If we do not make any such assumption and look simply at the facts, then we see that such reconciliation just does not take place, and that when there is said to be universal agreement this is simply a sign of universal oppression. Similarly, where what Dewey is calling 'personal culture', under which we might include personal criticism, becomes identified with social efficiency, it is because certain aims, certain requirements, have been imposed throughout society.

Dewey says that 'anything becomes an object of study when it figures as a fact to be reckoned with in the completion of a course of events in which one is engaged and by whose outcome one is affected'. (see chapter twenty). This means that study is incidental to carrying out practical work and covers anything that can be involved in such practical work. Dewey thus takes a 'practical' view of education itself. He supports 'learning by doing'.

In one sense that is a sound view: one learns mathematics by doing mathematics, by carrying out mathematical exercises. But that does not mean that one learns mathematics by, for example, fitting wall-paper, by serving some end external to the subject of mathematics itself. The 'learning by doing' approach ignores the interest in discovery, in the sort of outcome that consists in just knowing the subject. No doubt what I have called 'training in judgement' or, more exactly, the judgement that emerges from this training, can be applied to practical affairs, to one's occupation and to social life generally, but what it mainly contributes to is just the form of life which consists in the exercise of judgement.

I previously described intelligence as the recognition of the structure of a subject, and not the framing of a policy. Referring again to the *Republic*, we can say that the main difficulty encountered by the thinker returning into the Cave is just this demand that he should turn his views into a policy, that he should think in terms of what is to be done rather than simply of what is the case, or that he should think in terms of application as against the position that in the course of his thinking life he finds certain things out and this naturally affects what he later does. (A point of interest concerning the Cave is that its denizens treat things as separate objects, coexisting or in sequences, and their question is the utilitarian one of what will come out of the sequences rather than that of the characteristics or ways of proceeding of these objects.)

Dewey, like Huxley, thinks that certain policies or lines of action follow from the facts themselves. He speaks of 'the type of conduct demanded by facts', whereas the main relation of theory to policy is the negative one of showing that certain things proposed cannot be done. Theory does not show that certain things must be done. Such absolute demands are imported into or imposed upon theory. They have the effect of distorting theory. An example of this is Dewey's proposal of 'serving society', which carries with it a confused belief in the reconcilability of all social tendencies, as if there were only one type of social organization to be assisted, that is, as if assisting one did not mean hindering others.

These considerations affect Dewey's view of subject-matter, that is, of the place of particular studies in education. Thus, he refers to history and geography as 'the two great school resources for bringing about the enlargement of the significance of a direct personal experience'. He assumes that these studies lead pupils to participation in 'the life of humanity as a whole'. This might be thought to be in accordance with the view I have presented regarding the overcoming of the provincialism of time or space. But, in fact, it ignores the sifting process. It ignores the special kinds of activity in which communication is found, and it ignores the movements in opposition to such activity, movements which would prevent us from speaking in general of 'the world's work'. Thus, we find Dewey, in the chapter on educational values (Chapter XVIII), treating literary study as an ornament of study rather than its substance, taking it merely as one sort of appreciation alongside music, drawing, painting etcetera. This position fails to recognize the special character of literature as an embodiment or repository of culture, no matter how important music and art may be as parts of culture.

In the same chapter Dewey seems to give some recognition to qualities when he insists on the necessity of there being intrinsic values. But when we look into his argument, namely, that intrinsic values are implied by the very existence of instrumental values, we find that he does not get away from a relativist view: all he is saying is that if there are some things we want for what they bring about, there must be other things we just want. This is still relativist. It does not bring out the qualitative character of the lives in which various things are wanted. At the same time, the multiplicity of wants, and thus of the possibilities of personal development, cuts across the aim of social efficiency which Dewey would like to reconcile with personal development in education.

In Chapter XXIII ('Vocational Aspects of Education') Dewey opposes the extreme form of vocationalism, according to which education is training for a specific occupation, but he still thinks that education should be vocational in a broader sense. He thinks that it should train people for the variety of things that may occupy them in society, that the training itself should be of an occupational character, and that school life should be a kind of model of society. I have already suggested that such a course would weaken the definitely theoretical interests that pupils have. The emphasis on subject-matter gives an entirely different view of the nature of education from the emphasis on 'doing', which involves arbitrary and external ends.

One question that faces us here is, 'Is training in judgement itself in some sense vocational?' Of course, judgement is applicable to any vocation. But its standards of criticism are apt to cut across the current values of any occupation and to make one less inclined to throw oneself into that occupation. On the other hand, Dewey treats such training as vocational in so far as it leads on to certain kinds of career, for example, a scholarly career. He argues that the ordinary division between vocational and cultural is unsound, that it is really a distinction between types of vocation, not between vocational and non-vocational training, in which the word 'culture' has been restricted to certain kinds of career or occupation.

As to scholarship being a career, it may be that culture would not persist unless there were professional scholars. That does not mean, however, that the training of these scholars is training for a job, and it does not affect the fact that standards of criticism worked out in colleges of scholarship apply to all forms of life, so that education in this sense, even if it prepares some people for a special occupation, has a very much wider social bearing. Even those who are not going to enter such an occupation may come, through general cultural training, both to respect scholarship and to exercise criticism in their particular sphere of life.

Dewey's 'practical education', on the other hand, which is supposed to be a 'training for life' in which each pupil develops his own intelligence and aptitudes and at the same time learns to be cooperative, runs counter to the facts, as does his contention that by following his principles 'we may produce in schools a projection in type of the society we should like to realize, and by forming minds in accord with it gradually modify the larger and more recalcitrant features of adult society' (*Democracy and Education*, p. 370).

Here again we find Dewey's two major (false) assumptions: first, that 'we', the progressive teachers, have the power to plan a unified and progressive education, or that the school is so independent an institution as to be able to make for unity in the face of social division; and, secondly, that an insight into the social bearings of an occupation or into any social condition whatever shows that it can be improved, whereas it may show that it cannot be improved. A theory may show that things which some people want to have together are irreconcilable. This theory cannot be refuted by a mere demand, by a mere wish, for example, that 'personal development' and 'social efficiency' should be synonymous, when it is admitted that in the past they have actually been antagonistic.

7

University Reform

Reform of the university will be differently understood according as one starts from a commercial or from an academic point of view, and further differences will be occasioned by the acceptance of a solidarist or a pluralist view of society. It would appear, however, that even those who hold that the question is to be settled in terms of the university's 'ultimate value to the community', will require in the first instance to take account of the actual character of its work, and of its position as a special kind of social institution; they will have to consider the nature and conditions of *academic* activity or, at the very least, of 'research'. And even the most bigoted solidarist will hardly deny that institutions for 'the higher learning' have a history of their own and that, however they have interacted with other institutions, their development has been conditioned by an independent interest in investigation and has not been brought about by successive decisions of 'society'.

It is to be understood, of course, that the interest in investigation is not confined to universities, and, at the same time, that it does not function unhindered within them. But this merely means that, for those who are devoted to inquiry, university reform will consist in the strengthening of the forces of inquiry within the university and their closer alliance with similar forces outside, and that projected 'reforms' in any other direction are in reality reactionary. The point to be emphasized is that the adoption of either the solidarist or the commercialist position (and the two soon run together) can neither account for the origin of the spirit of investigation nor guarantee its continuance; subordinated to 'welfare' or to profit, science perishes. Certainly, the 'results' of investigation can be of great commercial value; certainly, the problems of industry can give an impetus to inquiry. But, unless the independent scientific spirit exists, such interrelations cannot continue—and, incidentally, in such a case industry itself will decline.

The first condition of the maintenance and strengthening of the academic spirit is publicity. This means not merely that the public should have information on university activities, but that the academic or cultural point of view should be propagated among the public. It is the business of academic investigators to speak out on behalf of their way of living and not, as is so often done, to apologize for it on the ground that after all it is of some assistance to non-academic enterprises. In this way they would not only arouse the cultural attitude in places where it is not at present active but would establish relations of solidarity with extra-academic investigators. They would aim, of course, not merely at enlisting formal support for culture but at carrying culture beyond the university. As far as present efforts in this direction are concerned, they have no more than an edifying, sermonistic effect; what is wanted is the encouragement of independent invesitgators, the organizing of groups of serious students, and (what all this involves) an active intervention in public affairs.

Even in a matter so closely, indeed essentially, related to university work as school education it is remarkable how unwilling university workers are to express themselves publicly on the subject, how strong a tendency they have to make it a matter of private conferences or even merely to accept the accomplished fact. It may be urged that an individual teacher is naturally unwilling to pose as the spokesman of the academic point of view; but it may be answered at once that unless academic workers are prepared to state what they *think* is the academic point of view, the academic point of view will never be stated. The notion that the interests of investigation can be served by official machinery, guarded by a 'hush-hush' policy instead of being ventilated by open discussion and criticism, is one that will not stand examination for a moment.

Clearly, the public propagation of the academic attitude will involve not merely support of certain extra-academic activities but also opposition to others—if only because of the strength of the anti-cultural tendencies in existing commercial society. The necessity of this opposition is very little recognized by university workers. Ignorant journalists and business men may make a cockshy of the university, but university men do not retaliate or, for the most part, even defend themselves. The academic view of the Press and of contemporary commerce could well be expressed in such terms as would shake up these vested interests, some of their more corrupt proceedings could easily be exposed by research workers—as apparently happens from time to time in the United States—but the university workers of the British Empire, at least, seem to 'know their place' too well to engage in any such vulgar controversies. It is unnecessary to enter here into the reasons for this state of affairs. But clearly what is needed first and foremost in the way of university reform is something that will stiffen the backs of academic workers, that will strengthen the academic forces within the university and make it function more actively in an academic way. It should not need further demonstration that, whatever may be the 'privacy' required for research, the academic life as such is not a secluded one, in the sense of being apart from social struggle. If it were, then, in these times, it could only perish.

For the reinforcing of the academic character of the university it is, of course, essential that the entrance standard should be maintained. The insistence on an entrance qualification which will be a guarantee of genuine cultural attainments, involves opposition to 'reform' along any of the lines currently suggested; for example, the provision of options in line

with 'up-to-date' (that is, business) requirements, the acceptance of schoolmasters' recommendations, or the substitution
of 'tests' for examinations in which candidates have to show an
ability to *discuss*—for it is above all in consecutive discussion
that the possession of a cultural background can appear. With
this is connected the serious question of the multiplication of
faculties. Here it may be contended that to bring within the
university studies which are generally pursued in technical
colleges of one kind or another, is to ensure that a high scientific standard will be maintained in investigations in these
departments; it may incidentally be argued that the first three
years' work in such courses as those in agriculture and veterinary science in Sydney University is substantially equivalent
to that required for a B.Sc. degree. Nevertheless, there is much
to be said for the view that the standard in all 'technical'
faculties would be improved if all students had to begin by
taking a degree in arts or pure science; and it may be added that
it would operate strongly for the advancement of science if
science students had a more thorough cultural training. At any
rate, it is worth noting that it is especially in connection with
the more 'practical' faculties that attempts are made to lower
the entrance standard. The strengthening of the academic
forces in the university, then, involves the renewed recognition of the central position of arts and pure science, as well as
the desirability of a closer correlation between the two; and it
involves, in Sydney, the restoration of the authority of the
Faculty of Arts in regard to conditions of entrance.

A further important requirement for the keeping up of
academic standards is an increased measure of control of universities by those who work in them. Indeed, it may be said
that, until universities are run by university staffs (with the
delegation of a share of responsibility for the conduct of their
studies to the students themselves), they will never be notably
academic. This, of course, would involve a tremendous alteration not merely in present forms of organization but in present
attitudes. It is remarkable that, though the governing bodies of

most universities are obviously ill-equipped for the management of educational activities, educational workers in their employment show the greatest reluctance to criticize their actions and policy, and especially to do it publicly. How this 'employee' complex can be thrown off it is not easy to see; but, at any rate, academic progress, if it does come about, will go hand in hand with the assertion by educational workers of their greater knowledge of the requirements of an educational institution than is possessed by the members of the legal, medical and other professions who are now in control. (Here, again, disunion and confusion of outlook are fostered among the staff by the multiplication of faculties.) One sign of a more vigorous attitude on the part of university teachers would be the adoption, by those of their number who sit on the governing body, of the policy of full discussion with their colleagues of the transactions of that body. Considerations of 'propriety' have little compatibility with a serious struggle for specific objects; and such considerations would soon cease to have weight, if university teachers became thoroughly convinced of the need for academic autonomy. The main force which may stimulate such a conviction is the growing invasion of the universities, and concurrent undermining of their authority, by business interests.

It is in connection with the question of university government that the proposals put forward by the officials of the recently formed Sydney University Graduates' Association are most strikingly reactionary. The suggestion that the present small representation of the staff on the governing body should actually be reduced is thoroughly in accordance with the desire to have a businesslike university (in which a clear line would be drawn between directors and employees), and it is not surprising that these reformers pursue their aims with the professed motive of 'service', which is the regular justification for every form of social interference. It is true that graduates *could* serve the university; they could do so by securing public support for the claims of academic independence, for the control of academic institutions by academic persons, in short, for the *democratic* working of these institutions. Indeed, with greater academic freedom, an increasing number of graduates would take this line. But, as it is, the generality of graduates have little understanding of either democracy or the academic life, and the above-mentioned proposal of a greater measure of external control is an illustration of this fact.

It may be urged that it is a reproach to universities if their graduates do not adopt a cultural outlook, and that this shows that some reform is urgently required. Undoubtedly that is so, but, as has been suggested, it is connected with the weakness of universities on the academic side and cannot be corrected by a further weakening in that direction. In particular, it is not to be expected that the products of the narrower professional schools would exhibit much interest in culture. But, even under the best of conditions, the mere possession of a degree would not be a guarantee of culture or, incidentally, of an understanding of how a university should be run. The question is not of the receipt of so much culture, which may then be retained as a possession, but of *ways of living*. Even in passing through the university a student does not necessarily become deeply immersed in the academic way of life; for the most part he has his professional prospects in view, and he remains apart from the permanent work of investigation, with which training for the professions is more or less harmoniously conjoined, but which no one will deny is an essential part of the university's activity. On the other hand, when he leaves the university, he does become immersed in a professional or commercial way of life, and may easily lose any sympathy he ever had with the academic life. Thus the notion that a graduate is fitted by his degree to contribute fruitfully to the working of the university is an entirely false one. It is well known that graduates' associations, particularly in the United States, have actively assisted in the commercializing of university life, and the same attitude appears in the Sydney proposals. The complaint that employers in general look askance at graduates is quite beside the point. There is little doubt that the main reason for this suspicious attitude is just that employers in general are opposed to freedom and grudge the university such freedom as it retains. And the notion that the university should alter its way of working in order to meet such complaints and suspicions is simply grotesque. As has been said, graduates in their professions and organizations and social life generally, could do something to propagate culture and stimulate recognition of the claims of the academic life; any graduates who do so may reasonably expect sympathetic cooperation from academic workers. But those who demand a hearing merely on the ground that they are graduates, are thereby showing their *lack* of culture.

Some remarks may be made here on the lecture system, on which a number of ill-considered criticisms have been passed. Obviously there can be good lectures and bad lectures—but it would be foolish to imagine that any system could be devised which would rule out the possibility of bad work. Tutorials and seminars could also be badly conducted, and there is nothing to show that they are bound to stimulate the student to more active thinking. Indeed, one might suggest that the demand for tutorials springs rather from the desire for an extended and more effective 'spoon-feeding'. If students think over the lecture-material for themselves and discuss it with one another, they will make more progress than if they are continually running to the staff for further explanations. The printing of lectures would not meet the situation at all; the question is of the gradual unfolding of a position and the growing understanding of it on the part of students—an understanding which is, of course, assisted by the working of class exercises, but which does not in any case keep exact step with the lectures, as if one should say, 'I have grasped that; what is the next step?' A further misunderstanding of the process of learning is shown in the contention that students cannot be intelligently taking in the material if they are writing all the time. Anyone with any experience of public lecturing knows how little is taken away by those who simply sit and display an 'intelligent interest', and how greatly understanding is enhanced by the practice of note-taking; he knows also how little intelligence there is in most of the questions asked 'on the spot'. There is no denying that improvement in many degree courses could be wrought, for example, by a reduction in the number of subjects to be taken, by an increase in the staff to meet the requirements of 'practical work', and by the provision of definite channels whereby students could express their criticisms of the courses they attend—such increased freedom for students being something that would naturally develop along with academic freedom in general. But lectures, whether in the form of presentation of unpublished material, criticism of published works, or simply the consecutive treatment of leading questions with which all students of the subject must come to terms, will always remain the central feature of any course of higher study.

There will, of course, be all the greater a tendency for students to think for themselves, if it is recognized that the university is not just a collection of professional training schools and, consequently, that the provision of lecture-courses is only one part of its work. The character of the university as an institution for learning will never receive due recognition, until those who are devoted to learning are prepared to uphold it as an independent social force, and to engage in a struggle *against* commercialism. Naturally, the representatives of academic autonomy will have to come to various arrangements with other social forces, but they will always get the worst of the bargain unless they make their independence a condition of the arrangements. This applies particularly to arrangements with the State. The university can demand State support on the ground that it does prepare for the professions and that it alone, precisely because of its disinterested approach to the questions involved, can do so efficiently. It follows, however, that it cannot accept State control of the administration of funds supplied by the State, or any State interference in its policy. The forces which go by the name of 'the State' do not understand the conditions necessary for the maintenance of academic standards, and have a definitely commercialist bias. Current proposals for examination 'reform', for the establishment of country colleges, and the like, illustrate these facts, and show the necessity for a consistent academic resistance to all attempts to *cheapen* education—which is the essence of the commercialist outlook. Only an aggressive policy can enable the university to maintain its standards in these times; and such a policy, with the greater academic freedom which it would entail, would stimulate the support of graduates instead of allowing them to drift easily into the commercialist camp.

The question of the university's attitude to the State is closely connected with the question of patriotism. It will naturally follow from the above considerations that the university cannot be officially patriotic or, at least, that, where it is so, it is departing from the academic point of view. In any department of political science, as well as in departments of cognate studies, patriotic and anti-patriotic views will be considered, and certain conclusions arrived at as to the working of patriotic sentiments in political affairs. But in an institution in which investigation is paramount, patriotism must be regarded as subject to investigation and criticism, and allegiance cannot be owed to institutions in which investigation is *not* paramount. The same applies to all questions of acute social controversy. In a developed university, Marxist and anti-Marxist views, religious and anti-religious views, the theories of Freud and theories opposed to Freud, will be thoroughly gone into, and the outcries of excited business men or anxious parents will be vigorously and not apologetically met. This means, as already indicated, that the upholders of investigation cannot keep their work entirely within the confines of a single institution but inevitably become involved in public controversies. In particular, they are forced to interest themselves in the whole educational system, and to support freedom of investigation in the schools as well as in the university. And, in general, their opposition to the subjection of the university to business interests carries over into every department of social life. It is an interesting fact, in this connection, that no considerable academic opposition to governmental censorship has hitherto been aroused; but what it indicates is the comparative weakness of the academic interest, the spirit of investigation, in the universities themselves.

It should always be remembered that culture is opposed not to commerce but to commercialism; the question is whether or not investigation is to be subordinated to the making of profits. As previously suggested, there is not only no opposition between science and industry, but the two are of the greatest assistance to one another. It was in Ionia as a centre of commerce that science first developed, and it is in the more industrially advanced countries that it still holds the leading place. But the mutual assistance between the two forms of activity depends on investigation not being subordinated to 'utilitarian' requirements. Indeed, the further development of industry at the present time depends on the passage from the standpoint of the consumer to that of the producer, from the disorganization occasioned by profit-seeking to the re-organization consequent on socialization. The attempt to impose a utilitarian outlook on the university is thus in line with the degeneration of present-day industry as indicated by unemployment, crisis and war. And, on the other hand, the upholding of academic standards is in line with the regeneration of industry by the productive forces which socialization will release.

It is not the object of this article to work out in detail the position here outlined. The point of immediate importance is that the academic forces are confronted by the forces of commercialism, and that the struggle against the latter can be conducted effectively only if the upholders of investigation take account of the general condition of society, the state of social forces and the direction of their movements. It is not enough that they should simply investigate; for the carrying out of investigation, the establishment of investigation as a way of life, depends on social conditions and involves relations of assistance and resistance to other forms of activity. And, of course, it is just because they are subjected to these opposing forces, because not merely the institutions they work in but they themselves carry the opposition within them, that investigators lose sight of the issues and have to be awakened, if investigation is to continue, to the dangers confronting them. But social orientation is precisely one of the conditions of culture; and thus we have another argument against narrow specialist training and in favour of the dissemination of culture, in the sense of a general grasp of the scientific, artistic and social activities of mankind, and the direction of one's own work in relation to these. The advancement of such culture, and that alone, is what can be seriously meant by university reform.

8

Education and Practicality

In connection with my criticisms of 'planning' and schemes of 'reform' (especially in the educational field) I have frequently been met by such questions as: What would you do if you were in charge of this or that institution? Aren't you ignoring the necessity for an administrative policy? How could things get done if everyone took the line of 'opposition'? Though the weakness of this type of 'answer' to criticism is a commonplace of logic, it may be worth while, in the present state of opinion, to make the main points again and to bring out some of the difficulties involved in the notion of practicality.

The position is somewhat similar to that which arises when criticisms are called 'destructive'. It is a device to avoid answering them in their own terms, that is, showing what is objectionable in their content, what they assert that is untrue. The notion of 'constructiveness' covers over the fact that to recognize the falsity of a received belief is to acquire knowledge. Of course, for the justification of a policy (or the proof of a conclusion) a universal proposition is required; and, in seeing the falsity of a universal proposition, we have as the object of our knowledge only a particular proposition. But still the justification of a policy is a theoretical operation, and there is no theoretical merit in clinging to a false belief; nor is it a defence of a particular policy, an answer to specific objections brought to it, to plead the necessity of having *some* policy. That plea is itself a piece of theorizing and has to submit to the conditions of theoretical inquiry—including the possibility of refutation.

It is especially to be noted that devotees of practicality make the voluntaristic assumption that things will not go on unless they are *made* to go on, and thus that, when a given policy is set aside without being 'replaced' by an alternative policy, the situation is so much the more anarchic. What is not understood here is the extent to which social activities and institutions are carried on by custom, without any formulation of a policy; so that the mere ruling out of a proposed line will mean that established ways of working will determine the event. This might, indeed, be called the 'policy' of falling back on custom, but that description would be misleading in that it ignored the distinction between formal decision and settled habit—and the fact that the latter plays a much larger part than the former in all human affairs.

There are, of course, a number of special assumptions that go with current voluntarism; one is that the general modern (and 'progressive') trend is towards an increase in conscious control, another that a new line (with decisions to implement it) is a matter of particular urgency at the present time. But both of these, in my view, are rooted in the main voluntaristic confusion noted above. And in any case both are theoretical assumptions and, as such, call for examination. This, however, is what the practicalist, with his plea of the urgent need for reorganization, is specially anxious to avoid; the urgency carries with it the need *not to discuss*. And when the theorist, for his part, says there is no hurry, he has in mind not merely the steady operation of custom but also the fact that the 'reformer' is to a large extent endeavouring to impose *his* customary ways of thinking and acting on other people. The 'urgency', the social 'crisis', arises, in fact, from an intensification of the opposition among ways of living; but that very condition makes the attempt to flatten out differences, to get an all-embracing policy, particularly malapropos.

This is connected with the practicalist's misunderstanding of the nature of administration; instead of taking it as a mechanism of adjustment among various competing and relatively independent tendencies, he takes it as *embracing* all special lines in a general policy of the organization or system. In other words, he is a totalitarian; and the totalitarian line, with the notion of the 'running' of things by some central body, is on the face of it no more practical, no more essential to the *doing* of things, than the line of adjustment among interests—in fact, it is less so, because the person or group attempting to control all particular activities is bound to be constantly making mistakes as to their possibilities of development. Thus the attitude embodied in the question 'What would you do (how would you deal with such and such a problem) if you were the government?' is idle, not merely because the very supposition of the occupation of a leading position by persons of your views implies that the problems would be quite different, but because governing does not mean imposing a solution from above and crushing opposition—because the opposition of the group or tendency you represent to certain policies is part of the problem. And the theorist who starts by asking what are the various interests involved is already much nearer a solution than the 'practical' man who simply asks 'What is to be done?'

The present is, of course, a period of the extension of State powers and is accordingly favourable to the conception of the 'running' of things from the centre; and, in particular, the invasion by the State of the *educational* field favours the development of schemes of educational organization and reorganization. But it makes all the difference to educational discussion if we recognize that it *is* an invasion, that the State does not create or own the interest in learning, that learning has its own history and traditions, and that in face of the State, whether as a special interest or as representing the current balance of social interests, it will operate to some extent as an opposition. And that means, under present conditions (though it may well be so under any conditions), that it will operate as an opposition *within* what are called educational institutions, that education in the sense of the development of habits of thinking will be struggling there with education (really mis-education) in the sense of the imposition of a discipline.

This being so, the problems of the free educator are no less practical than those of the *director*. He has to reckon with the restrictions which the latter imposes or attempts to impose. He has to face the certainty of hostile agitation if he sets about the teaching of history, for example, in a freethinking way; he cannot prevent the introduction of violently uncritical views into the very content of the educational process (for instance, the view that two warring groups of predatory powers one stands for 'justice'). It would be quite unpractical in that situation to refuse to have any truck with illiberal tendencies and regard any institution or course as educationally useless because illiberality flourished within it and even occupied the seat of 'control'. But that attitude would likewise be an *unthinking* one, ignoring the limitations of control and the operation of liberality in spite of it; whereas the truly critical mind feels itself to belong to a tradition, to be engaged in a set of practices, going back as far as education does.

The field of education, then, is a battlefield between liberality and illiberality—between cosmopolitanism and patriotism, between the treatment of the child as 'the heir of all the ages' and the treatment of him as job-fodder. And practicality, for the liberal, consists in keeping up this opposition, with the realization that while he can never get control of the system, he also can never be ousted from it. For any sort of education must involve a certain amount of freethinking; it must treat of certain *subjects*, and these cannot be completely canalized or directed to external ends—they must, to some extent, be developed in their own terms. Thus, while the contemporary attack on subjects and concern with the 'ends' of education are symptoms of educational decline, there are countervailing tendencies; and the person who thinks he can harness education to 'welfare' is unpractical, as well as untheoretical, in his misunderstanding of his material. A training dominated by the conception of utility, by the treatment of certain conditions of life as peculiarly *ends*, is a training in gullibility; but, in having any sort of subject-matter, it cannot entirely exclude criticism, even if it falls short in the *exposition* of critical method and the exposure of prejudice.

The practical policy of the liberal educator, then, is to extend critical thinking as far as possible—though, indeed, this may amount merely to saying that his 'policy' is *to be liberal*. And this will involve exposure of 'practicality', as embodied in the notion, prevalent even in universities, that there are 'practical' subjects, and that training in chemistry, for example, means the acquisition not simply of a knowledge of the nature of the subject-matter but also of ability to handle things in certain ways. It can, of course, be argued that the latter is essential to the former; but the 'practical' side of such courses goes far beyond the point which this consideration would justify. It is not, I think, Utopian to speculate on the possibility of a university which would be really liberal, in which all training would be training in theory, all subjects 'discussion subjects', all courses exercises in criticism; rather, it is informative, in so far as we can see this theoretical tendency struggling through existing obstacles. Perhaps we need never expect to see the university giving a course merely in medical *theory*, for example, so that its graduates could go on to junior positions in 'medical firms' (as law graduates enter legal firms) and learn their practice there. But such imaginings reinforce the point that practice is learned by practice and that the bulk of the 'practical' or 'professional' training of doctors, teachers and the like is quite useless.

One fundamental point in all this is that it is impossible to have a policy for everybody, that culture (in the sense of a critical attachment to the abiding forms of human achievement) is only one force in society, that it is confronted not merely by antagonism but by a widespread indifference. It is, of course, possible here to exaggerate divergences and overlook affinities. But at least it should be clear that education, in the sense of introduction to culture, on the one hand will never be the whole activity of 'educational' institutions and on the other hand operates vigorously outside them. The liberal will still endeavour to make them as far as possible an avenue to culture, a means of detaching students from the prejudices of their social milieu—of narrow-minded parents, for example, or guardians of 'morality'. But to ask him to have a policy also for the philistines, to have a scheme into which they can fit—that is entirely idle. They will be busy whatever he does; and he has enough to do combating them. Incidental to this combat, certainly, will be the making of compromises, of a certain composition of claims, in the institutions in which both sides are working; but the liberal will have no 'loyalty' to any such adjustment, he will continually seek a more favourable balance—recognizing, of course, that it is not always by frontal attacks that gains are made. And this, I contend, is a much more responsible attitude than any profession of caring for the interests of all, which means, in practice, a ruling out of liberality. Culture, it cannot be too strongly urged, is a special interest and requires, for its persistence, a certain irreconcilability.

9

Education for Democracy?

This[1] is the first of a series of pamphlets to be issued by the Australian Council for Educational Research, under the general title 'The Future of Education'. The series, Mr Medley tells us, is 'designed to emphasize the vital importance at the present time of devising a real plan of education for the future', and Professor H. Tasman Lovell, who as President of the Council contributes a foreword, expresses the hope that the pamphlets 'may prove a useful contribution to reconstruction'. It is clear that 'research' in the Council's view, is concerned with 'practical' problems, with determining what is to be done and not simply what is the case—clear, also, that this approach assumes what is *not* the case, namely, that we should all agree about what is 'desirable' (about what would be 'a better world after the war') though we may have doubts about how to get it. For if some of us do not share the aims of our educational reformers, we may attach no importance at all to any 'real plan' that they might devise. And while it may be impossible for anyone to discuss education without indicating to some extent what he supports and what he opposes, any research worthy of the name will take constant account of the controversial character of these questions and will give serious consideration to the social conditions determining the adoption of divergent views and programmes. If, as seems likely, advocacy is to play a large part in subsequent issues, the series

[1] J. D. G. Medley, *Education For Democracy*, Melbourne, 1943.

will contribute little to an understanding of actual trends in education.

The view that education is the key to society, that the way to have a better society is to have a better education, is plausible enough on the level of popular thinking, but one would expect professedly informed discussion to show some awareness of its difficulties and to provide some argument against opposing views—if only to the extent of considering disputes as to what is 'better'. After all, it is nearly a hundred years since Marx (third thesis on Feuerbach) attacked the conception of education as the agent of social change, pointing out the artificiality of the division of society into those who were to be improved through the improvement of their conditions and those who, presumably, had mastered their conditions and were to do the improving. And it was very little later that he and Engels, in the 'Communist Manifesto', criticized those Utopians who resolved history into the propagation and carrying out of 'social plans'. (The suggestion is, of course, in both cases, that the reformers represented a particular interest or way of living—and criticism of their professed disinterestedness would consist in showing what that interest was.) In fact, according to Marxism, social conditions not merely determine the adoption of views and programmes but determine what happens in considerable independence of what people believe and propose. Now the voluntarist may find it very hard to grasp this position, to see even what is *meant* by maintaining that the ideological struggle is incidental to a deeper social conflict; but, in view of the very great influence that Marxism has had during the past century, he may be expected to put up a case against it and not to ignore the doctrine of social struggle and the possibility of a class origin (or the colouring by some particular interest) of his own views. It is rather late in the day to be posing such simple questions as what 'we', in everybody's interest, shall do with educational institutions.

But, of course, these phenomena have to be looked at against the background of war, which puts Marxism, and social criticism generally, at a discount and gives an impetus to the voluntarist way of thinking. It is one of the aims of war propaganda to get people to believe that 'all this' is not to happen again and that it can be averted by eliminating or subduing ill-disposed powers and letting the well-disposed powers operate freely. The theoretical weakness of this position is obvious enough; the 'well-disposed' showed no capacity in the past for anticipating or controlling events, and the formula of 'eliminating the ill-disposed' does not on the face of it indicate any growth in competence, any deeper insight into world affairs. In fact, it is such as to cover the same advancing of special interests and ignoring of difficulties as led to the present turmoil. Yet, though critics may murmur 'The devil was sick', there are plenty of the uncritical who will accept the admonition to avoid 'post-mortems' and look to the future, who are eager for the new dispensation and so permit their rulers to absolve themselves from responsibility for present ills. That is one main condition of the spread of voluntarist ideas and the belief in 'goodwill' as the social panacea.

But that is only half the story. 'Reconstruction' propaganda is aimed not merely at maintaining present submissive attitudes but at facilitating future developments and particularly the trend, observable all over the world, towards centralization. To represent this as the approach to the reign of goodwill seems, once more, a highly implausible position, but it has its appeal to those who have become discouraged in the struggle to influence events and also to those who can envisage themselves as sharing in the work of 'guidance'—and these are the people who are most concerned in the propagation of the belief in a 'new order'. This is not to say that their activity is the chief factor in bringing about such an order; it can help to determine some of the details but in the main it is symptomatic of, and adapted to, a development which is taking place independently. None the less the acceleration of the tendency towards centralized control gives fresh opportunities to the devotees of guidance, gives them the chance in particular to put some of their rivals out of business, and this is in accordance with the monopolistic character of the whole process. Now if it were recognized that 'planning' means monopoly, it could not readily be associated with democracy or with 'education' in any sense other than regimentation. And it is here that the posing of the question in the form 'How shall we reconstruct?' has its usefulness—it covers over the critical question, 'What social interest does "reconstruction" represent?', and it prevents consideration of the view of democracy which historical determinism would oppose to the doctrines of the voluntaristic 'reformers'.

That view, taking its departure from the contentions that institutions have their own history and that this is a history of struggles, would take democracy to reside in the openness, the publicity, of struggle and not in devotion to a postulated 'general interest'. It would reject the conception of institutions as devices whereby people attain certain ends and maintain, on the contrary, that it is only *within* institutions that policies have any meaning. This is not to deny that institutions are interrelated, that other institutions are affected in special ways by political institutions, that there are important relations between publicity in society at large and publicity in such a special field as education. But whatever these relations may be (and the study of them has been greatly impeded by the Marxist reduction of all social diversity to a single conflict), the diversity and independence of institutions, and of interests operating within each institution, remain.

If, then, we consider the history of educational institutions themselves, we shall find it largely taken up with the struggle between the development of inquiry (education in the strict sense) and opposing forces which regularly come in the guise of 'social utility' and frequently take the form of State interference. And any attempt to enforce a view of what education shall be, inevitably interferes with inquiry. There can be fruitful (democratic) interaction between education and politics; it may be argued indeed (as I have argued elsewhere) that a

thorough education is necessarily political. But political training is not thorough unless it involves preparation for struggle
and criticism of the doctrine of social unity. A case in point is
the outrageous denial of educational facilities to Victorian
school-children who are not prepared to accept social unity
('loyalty') as a dogma. It will be argued, of course, that they are
accepting the protection of that which they refuse to acknowledge. But the question whether there is a protective
'system' or a conditional adjustment among divergent interests is just the matter in dispute. It is a greatly encouraging
sign, on the other side, that a majority of Australians have in
the recent elections refused to subscribe to a unity without
diversity, have shown some realization of the fact that agreement is only within limits and that a complete sinking of their
special interests ('putting their liberties in pawn') merely
means submission to the special interests of a minority.

As the reader will have gathered, there is no suggestion, in
Medley's pamphlet, of criticism of the doctrine of social unity;
'education in citizenship', 'learning the difficult lesson of
cooperation', are the burden of his song. He recognizes such
obstacles as timidity and laziness but has nothing to say about
the utilization of educational institutions in the service, of
special (commercial) interests. He involves himself at the very
outset in the vicious circle to which Marx drew attention.
'Any system of society—call it what you will—is no better and
no worse than the system of education which it fosters': so
runs his first 'general proposition'. Thus, to improve society
we have to improve education, but to improve education we
have to improve society. The assumption is, of course, that
there is a body of improvers who stand, as Marx put it, 'above
society', and presumably get their own education by revela-
tion from on high; but, if that is so, what becomes of the
'proposition'? And, if there were such a superior order, what
reason would there be for thinking that it would undermine its
position by 'the provision of a genuine equality of opportunity
for all citizens'? The error here lies in the notion of 'provision';

it is fashionable at present to counterpose equality and liberty, but, in fact, genuine equality depends on people's own efforts and is not something that can be bestowed.

On this question Medley himself is uneasy. Having outlined his scheme of 'real equality', distinguishing the pigeon-holes into which people may be fitted (he believes in 'vocational guidance', it need scarcely be said), he remarks:

It is easy to criticize the whole idea on the grounds that there will be no difference in fact between the society I have outlined and a totalitarian state. The difference can only be one of spirit—the spirit of man as opposed to that of the machine—and that difference can only be maintained by seeing to it that education in citizenship does not stop short with the school (pp. 24, 5).

So on p. 13:

What we must do is to realize now that the only difference between civilized societies in the future will be a difference not of social and administrative machinery, but of spirit—a difference between societies inspired by the spirit of man and those inspired by the spirit of the machine. It will be no use crying like children after spilt democracy. We must lift our eyes to a new order and see that it is one of our own making. If we resolve that it must be a democratic one, *we* must start here and now to *make our people* fit to have it, for if they are not fit it will not come to them (my italics).

Actually, the antithesis of spirit and machinery is a false one (like Lovell's antithesis of 'the nurture of persons' and 'the teaching of subjects', in the foreword); a particular spirit has its particular modes of operation, and the organization of an educational institution, for example, may be such as to kill or greatly weaken the spirit of inquiry. What Medley's 'difference of spirit' amounts to is a difference of name—regiment the people, have them all giving the maximum of service to the machine (not forgetting the extreme importance of 'physical education' and 'fitness'), but *call* the system 'democratic' and it won't be totalitarian.

The insubstantiality of Medley's 'democracy' can be made manifest by a few further citations. Having described democracy as a system in which a large majority of citizens play a significant part in 'the common business of the community', he goes on (p. 10) to give as his second general proposition, 'We are resolved that our system of society will after the war become a "democratic" one.' But then he says (p. 12): 'If my definition of a democratic society be accepted, it is clear that we have never been a democracy. It is clearer still that after the war we shall be even less of a democracy than we were before it'—which presumably means that there will be a *loss* of participation in public affairs. And this is illustrated, lower down, by the assertion: 'Peace must bring with it, if it is to be effective, an advance to a society based far more upon communal and less upon individual effort than has been the case in the past'—from which we might extract the sound conclusion that loss of independence means loss of democracy, though we might not call that 'an advance'. But then again, on p. 14, Medley informs us that 'We are not a physically fit people. . . . We are not a mentally fit people. . . . And all these things must be mended if our new democracy is to have a chance of existence.' What is to be inferred from all this except that our 'new' democracy will not be democracy at all?

That conclusion is reinforced by the further argument on p. 14:

Isn't it merely common sense to insist that a state which expects its citizens to play their part in its business should see to it that they are physically and mentally capable of doing so? And how can the state do this except by compelling them to become and to remain as fit as they can be both in body and mind? That is the only way to afford equality of opportunity and the only way to make our democracy possible.

It will make a difference to the commonsense of the matter if we conceive the state as concerned with the interrelations among many institutions or ways of living and not as a total organization of which they are subordinate parts (a view of an essentially militaristic character). And it is clear that that which exercises general compulsion is not that in which there is general participation but is a special interest of some kind. The kind of interest that requires physical fitness is not doubtful—and what can be meant by 'mental fitness' except submissiveness and adaptability to an allotted task? Could there be a more philistine way of describing the cultivation of the mind? But, if that is seriously in question, can 'mental fitness' be exhibited otherwise than in critical thinking? And can critical thinking be compelled? Does it develop otherwise than in independent institutions and, to a large extent, against 'the state', that is, as criticism of the system of rights which prevails at any given time, and in the attempt to force readjustment? Such opposition is in fact the condition of democracy, and the assumption of a total interest, or of a central organization which brings everything else under its wing, is anti-democratic. Neither democracy nor education can exist without controversy, they cannot exist without initiative, without spontaneous movements of the 'rank-and-file', and the greatest danger to both is the spurious agreement involved in submission to the 'expert', the official judge of 'fitness' and 'unfitness'.

The details of the scheme of 'equality of opportunity' do not matter very much. 'Reform' of the curriculum follows familiar lines.

There should be at school leaving age—say fifteen (plus)—a leaving certificate based on five main divisions—English, elementary mathematics, social science, general science and one other containing a wide variety of options. After it there should be retained in the educational system at the expense of the State wherever necessary all those who have any possibility of benefiting from higher education and they should undergo a two years' course of the kind which the Americans describe as 'orientation' or 'foundational'—(say) 50 per cent general subjects of a background character, 40 per cent preliminary specialist or technical training and 10 per cent physical, including if possible a period or periods in a labour camp engaged in manual work of national importance. At the end of this course—aged eighteen—those who have had all the higher education of which they are capable should be ruthlessly turned into the world, irrespective of their own desires or their economic position (p. 19).

One may question the use of the expression 'higher' here; at any rate, we still have control by the infallible expert and the very opposite of democracy. The development of democracy in the schools would require a freer, more critical treatment of existing subjects (particularly language and literature, as culturally fundamental) in which there is a coherent body of knowledge within the capacity of school pupils. But what sort of mastery of 'social science' can they have? Presumably the 'subject' would consist of odds and ends of information about the working of social and economic institutions, backed up by 'social unity' propaganda and sermons on 'citizenship' and 'fitness', that is, by the assumption of the very things a real social science would call in question.

The fate of universities is left a little obscure. It is suggested that professional courses could be made more 'humane', but at the same time

the idea that a technical education is in some way socially inferior to other kinds must disappear into the limbo of things best forgotten. Both tradition and convenience will continue to necessitate that certain branches of specialized training will be carried on in universities which, side by side with that training, emphasize the value of 'pure' knowledge and research as an essential accompaniment to any form of social progress. But the university of the future cannot arrogate to itself any monopoly of the educational stratosphere, and the sooner the problem of its proper relationship to the highest forms of what is at present called technical education is faced in a realistic manner, the better for all concerned.

In fact, 'the best contribution that universities can make towards "reconstruction research" is to start by reconstructing themselves in close collaboration with institutions of technical education' (pp. 22, 3). If they do, it is not hard to see their finish. If they adopt the criterion of social usefulness (in place of their own criterion of scholarship), they will very soon *be* technical institutions. The whole trend of Medley's proposals is in this direction; and it is the technicians who will constitute the 'educated élite' whose leadership he prefers not to call 'Fascism'. Presumably this is because no one will dispute it. 'It is in our conception of citizenship that we must find the foundation of our secular ethic and it is obvious that its main lesson must be the responsibility of every citizen for the community at large' (p. 24). And this conception is to be filled out by the activity of community centres. 'Goals cannot be reached without the machinery to attain them. A belief that talk is enough, that making speeches will itself produce results is a characteristic of democracy that has done us immeasurable harm. Let us cut the cackle and come to the community centres' (p. 26). The characteristic of democracy that Medley here caricatures is *opposition*; and the reality behind his idyllic picture of social agreement is the *repression* of opposition.

What I have tried to bring out in this review is the anti-democratic character of 'planning'. Much further argument would be required to show the illiberality of the reforming attitude in general. But I hope I have shown that the A.C.E.R. might well devote some of its 'research' to a consideration of liberality and utility as opposing trends in the educational world. Meanwhile it pleases me to think that this pamphlet so far gives the game away that it will do the cause of 'educational reconstruction' a great deal of harm.

10

The Future of Education

The first pamphlet in this series was reviewed in the last issue
of the Journal.[1] Subsequent numbers have not been sent to us
by the publishers; we have received the pamphlet under
review from the author, Professor Eric Ashby of Sydney
University.[2]

In the earlier review I drew attention to the character of
advocacy which seemed likely to attach to the series, to the
conception of 'research' as seeking to discover what is to be
done instead of what is actually happening, and to the insuffi-
cient emphasis placed on the *controversial* character of the
issues. My view is borne out by the general description here
given by the publishers to their 'Future of Education' series.
'The Australian Council for Educational Research is publishing, under the above general title, a series of pamphlets aiming
to show (*sic*) the need for, and to provide a plan for the
reconstruction of education in Australia.' It is implied that the
persons invited, as experts in some special region of educational theory and practice, to contribute to the discussion of
current problems, will all agree not merely on the need for
'reconstruction' but on its precise nature. We are perhaps to
suppose that so much research has already been done, and such
a body of basic principles established, that all that now remains
to be considered is *application*.

[1] See *Education For Democracy?*, the previous essay in this collection. (Ed.)
[2] Eric Ashby, *Universities in Australia* (The Future of Education, No. 5),
Australian Council for Educational Research, Melbourne, 1944.

But actual experience of the work of educationists, even without consideration of the very slight qualifications as 'researchers' in education of most of the contributors to this series, will very quickly show that this is not the case, that advocacy has characterized the movement from the start—in fact, that it is a *political* movement, and that the agreement in question arises not from research but from a common devotion to social uplift (involving, I should argue, a muddling of social categories, and catering above all for careerists). If the Council's aim is really to inquire into 'all phases of education and allied problems', it should give as much encouragement to *criticisms* of reconstruction (of the whole idea, as well as of particular schemes) as it does to 'practical' proposals for bringing it about. But especially it should consider 'problems' as *theoretical*, as questions of how actual events are to be accounted for. Once such explanations have been given, they may be utilized by advocates of quite different policies; it is quite wrong to assume that a specific line of action will follow from the facts, to imagine (for that is what it comes to) that there is only one 'end' which people can take the educational process to subserve. In fact, research could be quite usefully directed to a critical examination of educationists' notions of 'ends' and of the relation between theory and practice.

These points are illustrated in the pamphlet under review. It is marked by improvization, by a facile treatment of questions on which much solid thinking could be (and has been) done, and by the familiar conjunction of description with projects of 'reform'. At the very beginning Ashby disarmingly explains that he is addressing not his colleagues but the public—characteristically conceived as individuals with special avocations and wants, and not as participants in the movements and associations of cultural life. But actually the main points raised are of such a technical character that the ordinary member of the public could make little or nothing of them. What might appeal to him are the witticisms and catchwords and commonplaces with which the pamphlet is besprinkled and of which the following are examples: 'Given a good teacher sitting on one end of a log and an eager student sitting on the other end, the central problem of education is solved: you have the germ of a university.' 'Plato's *Republic* was written for his own satisfaction, not as a Royal Commission report.' 'Academic snobbishness is, of course, not unknown (many desirable reforms will be made only over the graves of some professors!)' 'The kingdom of the mind has its Munichs, too.' 'Faculties of Arts . . . must send into modern society graduates who appreciate values, not only in the context of the Parthenon and Pericles, but also in the context of greyhound racing and soap box oratory.' 'The good teacher prepares his class for ten or twenty years hence, when they will have forgotten all he is teaching them, except one or two guiding principles.' And then the answer to the 'practical man' who wants to know what use a graduate would be to him in the meat trade: 'I can only repeat that universities traffic in quality of mind, not merely in technical information: he knows as well as I that in the end quality of mind prevails over all else, even in the meat trade'. (A new meaning for 'quality butcher'.) I shall not disfigure this review by quoting the verses (by Mary Coleridge) which Ashby, in conclusion, takes as expressing 'the contrast between the impermanence of things made by Man, and the permanence of Man's thought, *formed out of dreams*' (my italics); it should at least be clear what I mean when I speak of improvization and the absence of hard thinking.

The affinity of Ashby's outlook with that of the A.C.E.R. is seen in the way he sets about his discussion.

In this essay I shall deal with the problems which Australian universities face to-day. They are problems which should be tackled now: for the future of this country depends on men and women; and men and women are slow to develop. If we want to produce sound citizens in ten years', in twenty years' time, we must begin now (p. 6).

There is no stopping to explain who 'we' are or what is meant by 'sound citizens' or why, out of a vacuum or in the midst of unsoundness, we must (or how we can) suddenly begin to produce them. It is obvious that there are unstated assumptions behind this fancied urgency, and what they are becomes more and more clear as the argument proceeds. For while Ashby endeavours to give an internal characterization of universities (a view of their 'essentials'), he constantly comes back to the question of the 'needs of society'. 'Provided a university is not disloyal to its tradition and does not lose sight of its purpose, it can, and should, shape itself to the society around it' (p. 12). 'Universities are instruments of Society' (p. 30); and, below, with reference to the contention that Australian universities are out of touch with the Australian community: 'The gravest [!] symptom of this is the gulf between the universities and the administrative arm of the Public Service.' Accordingly (pp. 32, 3), it is

the universities' duty to work out what sort of education a public service in an age of technology needs. The State is now a gigantic enterprise of engineering, chemistry, agriculture, economics. . . . It has been suggested in many quarters that as capitalism crumbles, so the administrators will inherit the earth. If they are to inherit the earth, it is the universities' business to see that they understand their inheritance.

Serving State enterprise—and finally being absorbed in it: that is the prospect which these considerations open up. It is because they adhere, consciously or unconsciously, to that tendency that the 'researchers' exhibit such remarkable unanimity; it is that 'imperative' which determines their assumptions and prevents them from seeing any force in criticisms of their 'practicality'. Ashby, of course, would like to make out that universities can keep their independent character while serving the State. But he gives no indication of having considered the difficulties of that view; and, if he were going into the question seriously, he would have to explain why the universities should not be found *opposing* the State or trying to *prevent* the administrators from 'inheriting the earth'.

The fact is that he assumes the 'unity' or reconcilability of all interests; and this means that, whatever he may say about the university's own character, his practical criterion, indefinite though it may be, is the 'needs' of society.

His account of that character illustrates once more the fact that solidarism (the doctrine of social unity) goes with individualism, the two being opposed to the pluralistic view of society as embracing many movements, which cannot be brought to any common denominator and among which antagonism is found—the State then being conceived as the adjustment which has temporarily been set up amongst them (or as the mechanism of adjustment), and not as the totality or system of social activities. The two essentials of a university, Ashby thinks, are that it is 'built of men' and that its aim is 'intellectual health'. Now it is obvious that there can be no universities without persons; but it is not at all obvious that 'the spirit of a university depends on the men and women who assemble there' (p. 8). As against this individualistic assumption it must be urged that institutions are prior to individuals, that they *form* individuals, determine the nature of their achievement and the heights they can rise to. It is false that the character of an enterprise is determined by the entry into it of men of a certain 'quality'; their quality is not independent of their work and their traditions. If the source of these traditions is a foreign one (as in the early stages of Australian university education), there must be some local tradition of a cognate character to enable the enterprise to get going at all. It is the quality it develops, when it does get going, which will determine whether 'first rate' men will be willing and able to work in it—and the question of 'cost' will be a secondary one. In fact, the academic quality is largely developed in the struggle against utilitarian tendencies.

Turning now to the second element, 'intellectual health' (a vile phrase, reminiscent of Medley's 'mental fitness'), we find that similar points can be raised in connection with it. Ashby refers here (p. 11) to Cardinal Newman, who confessed that he could not find a word which expresses for the mind what health is to the body and virtue is to the soul. 'Knowledge' does not express the idea, for knowledge is not a 'state or habit of the intellect.' 'Wisdom' is not the right word, for wisdom relates not only to the intellect, but to conduct and morality. It is this elusive quality of 'intellectual health', for which our language has no word, which comes within the scope of a university; this and this alone.

It is unnecessary to comment on this tawdry stuff in detail; it need only be said that our language has several appropriate words—one is *thinking*, another is *criticism*. But whereas 'intellectual health' clearly refers to some special quality of the individual, 'critical thinking' describes as much the quality of a school, the character of a tradition, as the activity of an individual. We can talk of a history of thought, a history of criticism; but a 'history of intellectual health'—that is plainly balderdash. Now if we say that a university is concerned to bring about *critical thinking* in its students (more exactly, that the academic life is a life of critical thinking), it is by no means apparent that it can 'shape itself' to the society around it without being false to its tradition; its essential attitude to society will be that of criticism. Moreover, critical thinking is clearly a moral activity, so that the antithesis of the cultivation of the intellect and the development of moral character is a false one.

Now no one will doubt that critical thinking can be exercised on all subjects; but there may still be certain special studies in which it is nourished. Ashby, then, quite properly raises at this point the question of curriculum, or of what *are* university subjects, but he handles it in a very indecisive way. 'Universities', he says (p. 13), 'are being pressed all the time to divert more and more of their resources to professional training, to satisfy the desires of modern society. But universities are concerned first of all with the *needs* of society, which are not the same as its desires.' It looks as if universities had more than one 'first' concern; and the point is scarcely cleared up by what is said a little later: 'I have described how universities began as professional schools and later discovered that their peculiar contribution to society was the culture of the intellect. They continued to train for the professions, but their real training was for adventure in the world of ideas.' Here 'contribution to society' is simply dragged in, and the utilitarian bias is reinforced by the conception of the university's primary function as training and not as the intellectual activity of its *permanent* members. I have not thought it worth while to examine in detail the sketchy account of the history of universities referred to in the last quotation, but it is pertinent here to remark that it completely ignores the Academy and all that followed from it.

Going on, then, to make this criterion more precise by reference to Whitehead's contention that 'the spirit of generalization should dominate a university', Ashby distinguishes between subjects which lead to generalization ('breed ideas in the mind') and those which do not, but borrow their principles from older studies. The latter are not university subjects, training in any of them 'is a technique, not an exercise for maintaining intellectual health', and while such training may quite properly be demanded, it is another matter altogether to demand it from universities. Of course, the university

has no antagonism to any kind of learning, technical or otherwise. *But its resources are very limited* (tenpence per head of population per annum in Australia): *accordingly it has to adopt a policy of expediency.* This policy demands that a great many subjects should be excluded from the university curriculum; the criterion I suggest will determine which these subjects should be (p. 15; my italics).

What a declension! What a *failure* to maintain a criterion! But it illustrates that element in Ashby's propaganda which makes it dangerous in a time of confused thinking, and that is its character of compromise, its having something for everybody. This 'advancing in all directions' is further illustrated in the succeeding paragraph (pp. 15, 16), which I think worth quoting in full.

I want to make this criterion quite clear, because there is a good deal of misunderstanding about it. Universities are accused of holding tightly to useless subjects and of hankering after the curriculum of their medieval ancestors. They are accused of neglecting useful subjects simply because they are useful. Now the criterion of a university subject has nothing to do with use or lack of use; it has only to do with intellectual content. When a new subject appears before the university for admission, the questions asked are: Does the subject breed ideas? Can research be done in the subject? Is it merely derived from other subjects? Never: Is the subject useful? There are still a few professors so bemused with medieval culture that they would like to drive out agriculture, commerce and the rest from the university, in favour of the trivium: grammar, rhetoric and logic. They are like the affected aesthetes of the last century who longed for the maypole and yule logs of Merrie England, and forgot the dirt and the stinks. When I assert that the university stands for the world of ideas and that its mission is to fight 'triviality, vocationalism and mediocrity', I do not advocate a retreat to the classics and philosophy, important as these are. In twentieth century Australia our prime need is to understand the twentieth century A.D., not the third century B.C. If it is properly taught, as much 'culture' can be put into a course on political science as into a course on Greek drama. Both subjects have a rich intellectual content. Both subjects involve the humanities. Both subjects are a training for intellectual health.

By means of the term 'need' Ashby manages to play fast and loose with the criterion of utility—but it is his real criterion, as is further indicated when he goes on to say that, while 'the faculties of "liberal" studies have lost sight of the needs of society', the professional faculties have not realized that the *best practical training* is the most theoretical one. If it had been said that the liberal faculties had fallen short in the *criticism* of society, that would have been a sound criticism of them, and one which could readily be linked with rejection of the doctrine of social unity implicit in such phrases as 'the needs of society'. For the recognition of academic independence goes with the recognition of independent social movements in general—of conflicting social interests, including interests opposed to learning as such. But Ashby's argument also glosses over corresponding conflicts within universities themselves. Increasingly influential groups do take the 'usefulness' of subjects and courses as a sufficient reason for their adoption for existing or new degrees, and it is *their* side in the controversy that is served by the insistence on up-to-dateness. This is only to be expected; it is, in fact, one of the conditions of critical thinking that it has to struggle with uncritical thinking, that there is no citadel to which it can retire and be secure. But that means that a university can never speak with a single voice, and it can be made to appear to do so only by a confusion of academic and utilitarian standards.

Now if we are to distinguish these two, if we are to see what academic standards are, we have to recognize that there are certain fundamental studies. No doubt it is possible in any subject to train in 'principles' rather than in technique, but such a training presumes a study of those *subjects* which have 'principles' for their content. Even the trivium, of which Ashby is so contemptuous, consists of subjects of quite general application. In particular, we can have a logical criticism of theories in the fields of agriculture and commerce, whereas agricultural or commercial criticism of logical theory would be merely farcical. How it is that logic (or philosophy) can operate in criticism of all theories and purposes, how it can concern itself with objectivity as such or set up absolute standards of judgement, is something that cannot be made clear without some penetration into the logical field itself. But even to pose the question sets it against the uncritical 'modernism' which would measure changing realities by changing standards, and allies it with classicism. If there are standards of judgement at all, they are permanent standards, and they will not, on the face of it, be grasped better in relation to contemporary than in relation to earlier conditions. In fact, it would seem that some knowledge of *varying* conditions would be of advantage for a judgement of what is permanent, as against what is merely current prejudice.

Thus when Ashby says (p. 18), after explaining that a classical education has not the same 'career value' in Australia as it has in Britain, that 'Faculties of Arts must still preserve and encourage classical studies: that is their obligation to the past. But Faculties of Arts, no less than Faculties of Medicine, have an obligation to the present', he completely misses the point of these studies. Their interest is not antiquarian; it is in standards of criticism that apply as much to the present as to any other time. What makes works and periods 'classical' is their objectivity, their demonstration of the ways of working of things themselves (of human and non-human *nature*) as against personal purposes and local requirements. It is not merely (though this is true, too) that with the passage of time special interests fall into the background and the achievements of disinterestedness more and more stand out; that would apply to the study of the past in general. But there have been conditions under which disinterestedness (culture) rose to extraordinary heights, and it is because classical Athens provides an outstanding example of this that it is especially worthy of study *now* or at any time—not, of course, to the exclusion of those 'classics' which crop up in modernistic periods like our own, but even so with a recognition of the considerable dependence of these later productions on the Athenian (or, more generally, the Graeco-Roman) tradition.

For while, in general, there can be no study of the present without study of the past, while we can be abreast of the questions of the day only by viewing them historically, it is especially in the classical age that we find the *foundations* of Western culture. It may be that schools of classical study have viewed the achievements of classical society in too narrowly 'literary' a way and so have not developed a sufficiently broad criticism of *modern* society—though even taking Ashby's facile antithesis of political science and Greek drama, we can say that the student of politics might learn a great deal from the works of Aristophanes, as well as of the tragedians. But what he has above all to learn from is Greek political theory; if that is not included in the range of his studies, he will simply be unaware of the source of many of his views and his judgement of contemporary affairs will be so much the more uncritical. The 'synthesis' of modern society which he is to get from 'a study of the social sciences: economics, geography, history, political science, anthropology, and so on' (p. 18), will be all the weaker because he is unacquainted with Socrates' criticisms of the 'synthetic' views of the modernists of his period, the Sophists. Even if what was wanted was a programme and not an intellectual orientation, the heaping together of particular studies, as against the search for their common foundation, would not be the way to get it. If critical inquiry is to go forward, then, it will be by *advancing* (not retreating) to 'the classics and philosophy', which alone can provide that foundation. In particular, as we have noted, this will be a basis for social criticism, including criticism of the judgement of universities by their contribution to society, as against the judgement of society by its support, or otherwise, of learning.

The remainder of the pamphlet is taken up with practical considerations, and here we can still observe the simple-minded character of Ashby's social views. Distinguishing (p. 20) between legitimate and illegitimate barriers to university education and taking the removal of illegitimate barriers to be the only defensible policy, he asserts that the 'chief illegitimate barrier is poverty'. Here he associates himself with the demagogy which has accompanied the proceedings of the Universities Commission, which, he considers (p. 21), has greatly lowered this barrier. 'By paying bursaries to students picked on merit, the Commission has to some extent excluded mediocrity and encouraged ability, irrespective of income level. This is the first step toward providing equality of opportunity in university education. Of course, it is only the first step', etc. It is, I say, a very simple-minded person who will imagine that the effects of poverty can be eliminated without the elimination of poverty itself—or, for that matter, that poverty itself can be eliminated. In the approach to any career there will always be facilities for the rich and difficulties for the poor. But, personal ambitions apart, it is *desirable* that there should be obstacles to overcome, that 'opportunity' should not take the form of a gift. And while the facilities referred to have a negligible effect on institutions of learning, while, indeed, their effect, as far as it goes, is in some ways beneficial in that students have a social background congruent with their studies, the effect of the Commonwealth's 'provision of opportunity' is thoroughly detrimental.

If the Commonwealth simply provided universities with funds which *they* could devote to the encouragement of needy students, there could be little objection—though it would be better that the universities should not be tied down to one particular form of the allocation of such subsidies. As it is, subsidised students are under a Government control which harasses them at every point, which puts them in their appropriate pigeon-holes and claims their later services, and which works towards a general control of universities. It is this policy which is served by the catchcry of 'ability v. mediocrity', and, in particular, by the treatment of entrance examinations, on which a rough but sufficiently accurate distinction of 'passes' from 'failures' can be based, as giving a reliable measure of ability all along the line—which involves a fetishism not only of marks but of ability, as if this were a fixed quantity, as if the sprouting of talent in an academic atmosphere were not one of the things on which a university should specially pride itself. And it is in support of regimentation, misnamed 'equality of opportunity', that we get such contentions as the following: 'A fit person, if he studies conscientiously, should pass the examinations and qualify for a degree without mishap.' 'The standard of examinations in Australian universities is no higher, and the level of teaching is no worse than in British universities; but failures in Britain are less common. *Therefore*, the qualification for entrance must be too low' (pp. 21,2: my italics). Much of this is merely tendencious dogma. It is surely a very narrow view which takes conscientious study as the sole mark of a student's profiting by his participation in university life, and insists on graduation in the minimum time; and the 'therefore' covers a very hasty ruling out of other explanations of failure—particularly, bad schooling. The principle dictating such arguments is simply 'social utility'—which has acquired a peculiar sanctity in its present form of 'national service'.

Little can be said, it seems to me, in favour of Ashby's other projects of reform. I should regard the statement that 'you cannot treat a class as adults when sixty-eight per cent of them are no older than seventeen' as simply false; and, even if it were true, it would not settle the question of the degree of maturity to be expected of students at entrance, of the extent to which they should mature within the university itself. But it is interesting to observe that Ashby supports his view by reference (p. 23) to the suggestion of the Committee of the British Association on Post-War University Education that 'the "modal" age of entry to universities should be not less than nineteen, preferably after a year of approved national or international service'. ('Or international' is the cream of the jest.) On the other hand, I see no force in the contention that the student's whole life should be taken up by his membership of the university, and the analogy by which Ashby reinforces that view strikes me as singularly inept: 'An army which trains from nine a.m. to five p.m., five days a week, thirty weeks in a year, would make a poor show in battle. Yet we are satisfied with this part-time training for the defence of the kingdom of the mind' (p. 22). The student's independence (among other things, as an inquirer) is fostered by his participation in various institutions, and the unfree conditions of military service have only a negative bearing on the conditions of intellectual development. The 'kingdom of the mind' fares badly when it is treated as a separate world and when students and teachers do not make vigorous incursions into political and social life.[3]

The supreme example of hasty argument, however, occurs on p. 31, where Ashby is treating of the relation of the universities to the Public Service. 'We expatiate on the need for equality of opportunity; we demand a university education for all who matriculate. Therefore we apparently set a high value on education. On the other hand we set a high value on service to the State: no school speech day is complete which doesn't mention citizenship, and the need for our best brains to serve the country. We cannot have it both ways: either the entire educational system of this country is built on a fallacy, or the Public Services should be recruiting men for administration from the universities.' Actually it is Ashby who is committing the fallacy—the commonplace fallacy of undistributed middle. He is arguing that it is inconsistent to put a high value on education and on public service, and not to see to it that public servants are educated. Formally, then, the argument runs: The educated are valued, State servants are valued, therefore State servants are educated—for if they are not, that shows that we do not really value one or other of the classes in question; that is, if the conclusion is false, at least one of the premises is false (another way of saying that the argument is valid). Incidentally, if consistent adherence to these valuations required that State servants should be educated, it would equally require that the educated should be State servants—a highly significant point in view of the political characterization of the

---

[3] It might be thought that this would be partially achieved, as far as students are concerned, by Ashby's proposals (pp. 27, 8) for 'migration' between Australian universities. But, though there might be little harm in such a scheme, there would be little point in it. It is not by travelling about that a student will become possessed of 'cultural wealth', the criterion is not extensiveness (cf. the 'social synthesis') but intensiveness, and this might well be hindered by 'migration'. It would certainly be prejudicial to this essential characteristic of university study to 'coordinate' courses and examinations in the different universities, for the sake of the migrating student.

'reforming' movement given earlier in this review. There is, of course, no ground for arguing that, if we value two things, we must amalgamate them; there is no inconsistency to recognizing distinct kinds of merit ('good brains') and in holding, for example, that administrative brains *are not* speculative brains, though this would be nothing against the existence of common features, and even a common part, in the training of the two. It may also be remarked here that, whatever interests may be served by the humbug of 'speech day', the distinguishing-mark of citizenship is not service but the right of opposition.

In the foregoing discussion I have in the main followed the order of Ashby's exposition, but I have reserved comment on the section (pp. 23–27) dealing with decentralization of universities. This seems to me to be much the most vigorously argued part of the pamphlet, the only one, indeed, in which Ashby is really at home with his theme. In the essay as a whole, theory and policy, the exhibiting of the character of university work and the advancing of 'reforms', trip over one another. No doubt this sort of confusion is inherent in the reconstructive mentality; in any case, clarity would require that the former matter be dealt with independently of plans and policies, and, in regard to the latter, that a general political programme be presented with no special emphasis on education or, perhaps better, with correlation between educational and other (especially industrial) planning. But in decentralization we have a practical problem, that is, one in which the implications of various policies can be estimated and compared, in the first instance against a background of academic assumptions but perhaps also in such a way as to bring the main issues home to non-academic persons. If this had been taken as the subject of the pamphlet, if the points raised had been developed more fully, with special consideration of the objections which have been or might be brought to the views adopted, that would have been a solid contribution to the discussion of educational prospects. As it is, the discussion of decentralization suffers not only from its brevity but from being embedded in the larger and looser discussion I have been criticizing.

The summary character of the discussion is particularly noticeable in the remarks at the outset on whether the expected influx of students after the war is to be met by increasing the size of universities or by creating new establishments.

On the one hand it is maintained that Sydney and Melbourne, with three or four thousand students, are too big; expansion should, therefore, be through university colleges outside capital cities. On the other hand it is maintained that until we can provide better staff and equipment for the universities we already have it is bad policy to dissipate our limited resources on what are certain to be third rate colleges (p. 23).

Ashby thinks it easy to demolish both sides of the argument, but does nothing towards that demolition except to give a few illustrations from overseas practice; and with the assertion (p. 24) that the 'bulk of academic opinion favours some decentralization of tertiary education, in order to stimulate local interest and because it is absolutely essential to abolish the mass teaching of first-year students', he proceeds at once to his main problem, what is to be the character of the new establishments.

But it should be noted that he has misstated the case of the opponents of new establishments; the point is that, under most circumstances, it is good policy to put available resources at the disposal of existing universities because it enables them to give a greater variety of courses, to institute new lines of study, as against the conducting of studies of the same sort in different places—a point to which Ashby makes some concession in his further discussion (p. 25) in preferring to such duplication the institution of bursaries enabling country students to come to the city. Of course, there are conditions where a growing provincial centre may properly set up its own university, but nothing has been said to show that these conditions exist in

Australia. In fact, in deliberately setting aside the question of new universities and concentrating on the question of 'colleges' of one kind or another, Ashby would appear to be aiming at a compromise with existing forces, whose character and tendency a more thorough consideration of principles might show to be anti-academic. At any rate, his judgement as to the 'bulk of academic opinion' is discounted by the fact that academic opinion has not had the chance to consider the question fairly and fully, and that it has largely resigned itself to being confronted with decisions which it has had very little voice in determining. It will be time enough to talk about academic opinion when universities are run by the people who work in them, though even now I very much doubt whether a plebiscite of professors would confirm Ashby's claim.

As to the size of first-year classes, the problem can be dealt with (as in many universities) by dividing such classes into sections; and, whatever inconveniences this may involve, it is at least better than separation into different centres, in that the student is brought into some contact with the work and life of a well-established university; moreover, the additional members of staff required by this system will not spend all their time with first-year classes, and a general strengthening of departments may result. More generally, the problem of numbers might be settled by separating professional schools from the university, perhaps even establishing them in country centres. This would be obviously suitable in the case of schools of agriculture and veterinary science, admission to which could be by the university's B.Sc. degree—perhaps with a recommendation to candidates to include certain subjects in their science course. It would no doubt be Utopian to look for a throwing off of B.M.A. influence and the setting up of a degree in pure medical science, the university not concerning itself with the professional courses to which this might lead up. At any rate, proper consideration is not, in my view, being given to the subject unless the question of the over-professionalization of universities is taken up.

Ashby, however, concentrates on the question of colleges, and develops his argument around the distinction between a 'vertical' and a 'horizontal' cleavage among institutions preparing students for a degree. A vertical cleavage is one in which the same ground is covered in several places—though it is surely misleading to make it a question of the covering by the new college of 'the whole gamut of the mother university, up to pass and honours degrees and post-graduate work'; there might still, under any scheme of decentralization, without difficulty as to numbers or 'local interest', be some types of work that were done only in the centre, and particularly it might remain the *post-graduate* centre. On the general question of 'daughter colleges', then, Ashby asserts (p. 24) that if their students

are to enjoy the privilege of degrees from the mother university, the mother university must clearly control the curriculum and examinations. This means that the college teaches (or crams) for an external degree, and that the student writes after his name the imprimatur of a university he has never attended. Since the passing of examinations is only one ingredient of a degree (according to some, the least important ingredient), there is a serious risk that the currency of the degree will be debased.

(It will be remembered that the securing of a degree in the minimum time was earlier taken as a criterion of 'fitness'. And while this might conceivably be a necessary though not a sufficient condition of profiting from a university course, it is fairly obvious that immersion in other forms of university activity can lead to a student's failing in some of his examinations.) There would, of course, be such a risk, but it would presumably be even greater in colleges which were not organized after the same plan, and had not the same purposes, as the parent university. The 'vertical' college, if its staff were appointed by, and kept in touch with, the parent university, might be expected to develop a similar outlook. And there is at least a parallel between the university's conducting of the examinations and a professor's examining of students on a course given by a lecturer.

We are apparently to understand that in the case of 'horizontal' cleavage, where a college does *part* of the university's work or does work taken as equivalent to part of the work of a degree, there will be no such central control. Under such conditions, it seems to me, standards would inevitably be lowered; at any rate, to say that we can arrange, *'with the necessary safeguards*, for some work done at approved teachers' colleges and technical colleges to count towards a university degree' (p. 27; my italics) is to beg the question of the existence of *any* safeguard other than university control. It is also somewhat staggering to be told, out of the blue, that where necessary junior colleges can be set up in country towns 'under the State Department of Education' (p. 26), no other type of control of junior colleges being anywhere suggested; this is not very promising for standards. One might sympathize with Ashby's parallel suggestion for the development of 'post-matriculation work' in schools, though there might be considerable doubts as to what exemption (if any) from university courses this should give, and though, again, the picture of the painful impact of the university on the schoolboy entrant seems to me grossly overdrawn. But, in regard to colleges, Ashby's argument gives the impression that he has looked for objections to the 'vertical' system and for considerations favourable to the 'horizontal' system—more generally, that he is presenting us with a piece of special pleading in support of a fairly complete scheme on which he has made up his mind, and not with such a canvassing of principles as will open up discussion and lead to an exploring of possibilities.

A word might be said in conclusion on the footnote which appears on the opening page of Ashby's essay: 'The opinions expressed in this essay are those of the author. It must not be assumed that they are the opinions of the Governing Body of the University in which he serves.' It is the misfortune of Sydney as of most other universities to be subject to the nominal government and the real interference of an essentially non-academic body. But it is strange that an academic worker, making public pronouncements on questions of the greatest academic importance, should think it necessary to guard against compromising such a body, even if he happens to be a member of it, and even if it has or is developing a policy on the 'college' question. This attitude, in my opinion, compromises the cause of academic freedom.

11

Art and Morality

The agitation against the recent prohibition of the importation of James Joyce's *Ulysses*[1] into Australia did not last long; indeed, there was scarcely a protest when the Labour Minister for Customs confirmed the verdict of his predecessor. This, it may be said, is not surprising in circumstances of national emergency—people have more urgent matters to attend to, and there will be time enough, when peace is restored, to take up such special questions again. Now, while the question of culture in war-time is one which might profitably be argued much more fully than it has hitherto been, it is not my purpose here to go into that question. But there is, I think, an interesting parallel between literary and political censorship, between attacks on the 'obscene' and attacks on the 'seditious' or 'disloyal'.

While the main point of war-censorship is understood to be the prevention of the giving of information to the enemy, there is no doubt that very considerable limitations are placed, by censorship as well as by other means, on the expression of political opinions—in particular, those judged to be unfavourable to the national cause. And one implication of this is that the 'national cause' has already been defined beyond dispute. In the same way, in professing to speak 'in the name of morality', the supporters of the ban on *Ulysses* assume that their conception of morality is one that all must accept. Their

[1] James Joyce, *Ulysses*, Paris, 1922.

position would obviously be weakened if they admitted that they were speaking only in the name of *a* morality, if they had to uphold what we may call the morality of protection against the morality of freedom. To do so they would have to rest their arguments (in so far as they do argue and do not merely indulge in noisy denunciation) on some common ground —though this, to the same degree as it facilitated discussion, would make banning more difficult.

Indeed, the more we examine the position of the censors of the morally or politically unorthodox, the weaker do we find it to be. It is obvious that the orthodox view has immense initial advantages; and if those who support it do not want opposing views to be even stated, this would suggest that they doubt its ability to hold its own in free debate—from which it might further be inferred that the view they promulgate differs in important respects from what they really believe. Again (as has been regularly pointed out in discussions of this sort), they imply, in professing to be able to censor, that they themselves will take no harm from examining what they proceed to suppress; in other words, that there is a line of social demarcation between protectors and protected—a line which, since it is drawn by the protectors themselves, will always seem highly arbitrary to those who do not unquestioningly accept protection.

It is here, of course, that we are met with the plea of urgency—irreparable harm may be done while the question is being debated; even if in the end those who proclaimed themselves competent are shown really to be so, it may be too late; the 'enemy' may have gained a footing from which he cannot be ousted. Here we have the doctrine of the 'fatal attractiveness' of falsehood and evil. Though certain positions can be conclusively demonstrated, immature minds will rush to the contrary positions as soon as they are confronted by the problems. Accordingly, they should be subjected to authority; they should be kept away from these problems as problems, and be presented only with the solutions.

The glaring weakness of this position is that if moral or political 'minors' could be kept away from the problems, if these were something merely external to them, there would be no fatal attraction. It is because sexuality is part of the child's make-up, because the tendency to enterprise is inherent in the worker's social position, that 'indecency' and 'subversive' doctrines have so strong an appeal. And in keeping these things down, in seeking to abolish what arises in the nature of the case, the protectors are not merely falsifying the facts but are showing that they themselves have special interests, that their 'protection' embodies repression and exploitation. In a liberal régime 'subversive' tendencies are intellectually exposed and refuted (while, of course, considerable heterodoxy is tolerated); in an illiberal régime where, from lack of freedom, they are more deeply rooted, they are physically repressed.

One does not, of course, expect to find a purely liberal or democratic régime; but a régime, in so far as it is democratic, supports open discussion and, in so far as it censors, is anti-democratic. Censorship 'manufactures the evidence' of social solidarity. It produces *some* of the features of intellectual agreement, but a very different spirit is manifested in the two cases. Those who have come to terms with conflicting views and tendencies are far more vigorous and able upholders of a cause than those who simply follow authority; the latter are divided in mind and prone to panic, the former are adaptable and enterprising. At least, it should be clear that the question is not of the 'defence of morality' but of the existence of conflicting moralities, the morality of defence or protection being opposed by the morality of enterprise or initiative, according to which not having tackled problems directly, not having been subjected to 'temptation', is a moral defect, a disqualification for responsible living. From this point of view protectors and protected alike exhibit a *low* morality; there is no moral elevation without open discussion. And literary elevation is one particular case of moral elevation. Just as 'the only check that ought to be placed on literature is criticism' (A. R. Orage), so good literature is itself critical and revealing, and protective literature, the literature of comfort and consolation, is bad.

But, whatever the detailed differences may be, the first point to be made is just that there are different moralities, opposing sets of rules of human behaviour. This is because there are different ways of life, different 'movements', each with its own rules of procedure for its members. Such rules, it may be noted, need not have been formulated; but the more important point is that, formulated or unformulated, they are not to be regarded as preceptual or mandatory. We speak of 'laws of nature', but by this is to be understood the ways of working which things themselves have and not anything imposed on them from without, anything which they 'obey'. In the same way, the moral question is of how people do behave and not of their 'obeying the moral law'; obedience, or the treating of something as an authority, is just one particular way of behaving, the moral characterization of which has still to be given. The phrase 'how people do behave' may be misleading here. It is not a question of taking any type of activity in isolation; we do not have a morality until we have a way of life, a number of ways of behaving that hang together, that constitute a system—and it is in the conflict of such systems that rules come to be formulated. From this point of view it might be best to say that a morality *is* a way of life or a movement; and in that case the person who spoke in the name of 'morality' would be neglecting to specify the movement he represented.

That, at least, is one defensible usage. Alternatively, we might identify morality with the preceptual system, with living in obedience to authority—or, admitting that there are many authorities, we might speak of many moralities, while recognizing that there is also a movement, a way of living, which rejects all authority but still has its own character (or, again, we might recognize many 'free' movements). The multiplicity of authorities, however, is just what the authorities will not admit; each sets itself up as *the* authority, as laying down what is absolutely mandatory, what, in the nature of things and not relatively to any particular movement or director, is required of people. To speak on behalf of morality, in this sense, is to speak on behalf of the principle of authority—and so again (whatever the actual power may be that is thus metaphysically bolstered up) to support a low way of living. It is low, in particular, because it is anti-intellectual, because it is necessarily dogmatic. Some account can be given of the relation of a particular 'rule' or way of behaving to a certain way of life, but it can have no demonstrable relation to 'the nature of things'. To say that something is required by the nature of things is just to say that it is required—to say, without reason, that it 'is to be done'; and, as soon as any specification is attempted, the whole structure breaks down. If, for example, we are told to do something because God commands us to do so, we can immediately ask why we should do what God commands—and any intelligible answer brings us back to *human* relationships, to the struggle between opposing movements. In that region, to accept authority is simply to bow to superior force; but it eases the situation for both oppressors and oppressed to represent this as bowing to some Absolute, to the authoritative as such—in other words, to the unintelligible.

This does not mean that reasons can be found for everything we do; it can be shown that a particular line of action contributes to a more general form of activity, but such considerations of policy always lead back to activities for which no reason is sought, to activities in which we are actually engaged. In fact, ways of life are prior to policies, they *frame* policies, and, while different ways of life may have sufficient in common to permit of some compromise, some working arrangement, it constantly happens that what suits one does not suit another, that what from one point of view is a reason is from the other no reason at all. All they can do, then, is to fight it out—even the compromise depends on the exertion of a certain force by the various parties to it—and the struggle between different ways of life may be taken as the outstanding feature of social existence. But what the authoritarians, the 'moralists', maintain is that their reasons are 'essentially reasonable', that they are of a higher order than those of the non-authoritarians, and in this way they seek to disarm their opponents. The argument is of an ontological character; that which is binding-in-itself must have greater force than that which is not, just as that which exists-in-itself must be stronger than anything which exists under certain conditions—and ceases under certain conditions. And the freethinker is made to appear to be putting that which depends on something else above that which depends on nothing else, when he is really saying that there is no such thing as the latter, that the conception of the non-dependent is a confused one. Though this type of authoritarian argument (whether in its classic form, dealt with by Kant, or in more special forms) has been refuted again and again, it still imposes on the weak-minded; but even they would begin to see daylight under conditions of fair intellectual fight, and that is why authoritarians invariably add censorship, preventing arguments from being even heard, to intellectual crookedness.

The main point is the close connection between the upholding of a hierarchical doctrine of reality and the maintenance of a *social* hierarchy. And though, as already noted, we can distinguish various authoritarian movements (though there are different views of the proper order of the layers in the social pyramid), they all come together in this, that they recognize *some* order, that they deny the necessity or naturalness of conflict, that is, that they take a solidarist view of society; and thus it is that, in spite of superficial differences between them, they are regularly to be found working together in opposition to 'disorder'. The accusation that he is upholding privilege and servitude is, of course, one that the ordinary solidarist would indignantly repel, since he is maintaining that all are equally partners in the social concern; but it is by this very pretence at equality (as far as it is made plausible) that inequalities are covered over and the unprivileged are detached from the independent movements which are their escape from servitude. In fact, philanthropy implies inequality; it is 'relief' given by the privileged to the unprivileged, but it leaves privileges as they are. The best intentions in the world will not succeed by such methods in *bringing about* equality, in bringing the lower orders up to a higher level; it is by what they *are*, not by what they are given, that men will win release from servitude. If the philanthropist were really going to assist those he professes to be interested in, he would join their movements, he would *be* one of them. But he is not; and his philanthropy (his good intentions, his self-righteousness) is merely a means whereby their movements are weakened. It is curious that the philanthropic ideology is what nowadays passes as 'socialist', but its purpose in its new setting is the same as that of ordinary bourgeois philanthropy, to pass off a hierarchical system as egalitarian, to sidetrack on the one hand, and on the other hand to justify the repression of, those independent movements which would alter the balance of social power.

Now all this is highly relevant to *Ulysses*. The position taken up by Joyce (as Stephen Dedalus) is above all a refusal to *serve*, a rejection of despotism, however benevolent its guise, a rejection of the master-servant relationship (with which is bound up the whole ideology of utility and social service), and hence a rejection of theology. More exactly, we are presented with Stephen's mental struggle against servitude, a servitude imposed upon him by the submission of his country to 'two masters . . . the imperial British state and the holy Roman catholic and apostolic church'—and hence a struggle against Ireland itself, though this is something from which he can never be wholly free. To the bowelless critics of the book, steeped as they are in servility and easy social compromise, this struggle means nothing—and so they fasten on incidentals: the grotesqueries of style, the printing of the 'unprintable', the general 'unpleasantness' (that is, the fact that the portrayal of any real struggle does not comfort and console). But, for the

'intellectual imagination' of Joyce, the makeshifts of the
bourgeois world, and of the well-ordered universe which is its
theological counterpart, are intolerable.

It is idle, then, to call Joyce 'blasphemous'; that is only to say
that the battle should not be fought—it is no answer at all to
Joyce's intellectual attack, to his bringing out of the human,
the servile, content of theology. His 'free thought' consists, in
the first instance, not in rejecting theology, but in taking it
quite seriously. If there *were* a master of the universe, then
Joyce, to the extent of his power, would fight against him; he
will not endure servitude, he cannot accept sacrifice and
atonement, he rebels against the low conception of life, the
base morality, which they imply. And this means that he is
considering them in human terms (these being the only terms
in which they are intelligible), that he recognizes the arbitrari-
ness of 'analogical reasoning', of the mystery-mongering
which makes such things partly human and partly non-
human. 'With me all or not at all.'

Ulysses, of course, is not a work of science. Dedalus works
out no Feuerbachian reduction of the divine world to the
human. Nevertheless, that is what is involved in his soul's
crisis in the book. It is institutions, earthly authorities, that
impose servitude in the name of heavenly authority. And it is
the earthly content of theological conceptions that alone has
psychic and social importance. 'My hell, and Ireland's, is in
this life.' Hell, the self-alienation of the spirit, occurs here and
now; it is something that has to be fought through, not something that we can avoid by propitiating human or 'cosmic'
powers, not something that we can be protected from. He
who remains in the circle of propitiation and protection
remains in hell. He alone works through it who rejects the easy
ways of escape—nodding at an image, repenting, letting one
thing 'stand for' another—the whole system of anti-
intellectual pretences. This is the central theme of *Ulysses*, and
it is this that the Homeric material (the descent to and return
from the shades, contentment with a swinish existence,

mock-heroism and so forth) subserves. And it is because the theologians cannot meet this intellectual attack, while at the same time they wish to keep up the pretence at intellectuality which theology is, that they take refuge in accusations of blasphemy and immorality, of damage to immature minds—when in fact the issue raised is whether the life *they* uphold is not death to the spirit and when Joyce's free speculation is setting itself up as a *morality* (in the first sense suggested above), as a way of life opposed to precept and protection (which, as we have seen, is above all the protection of vested interests).

Actually, *Ulysses* would produce little or no effect on the immature; it is a book for the mature, but not for the servile, who are shocked by it because it confronts them with a freedom they have lost, because they can no longer face unpleasant facts and particularly their own defeats, because it attacks the ceremonial and fetishistic system by which they conceal these things from themselves. And because the immature have not yet been defeated and might come to see through the prevailing pretences, their guardians are anxious that they should not learn that anything but the ceremonial system exists. It is noteworthy that what they are not to hear about is above all *sexual* transgression; this is what 'immorality' has come to mean. Our censors do not say: 'this book portrays spite, that book portrays tyranny and greed, therefore children must not read them in case they should become spiteful, tyrannical and greedy.' There is a general understanding that in a proper book evil conduct meets with some punishment; but, for the most part, such faults are not even noticed, and they are certainly not taken to be contagious in the way that *sexual* impropriety is supposed to be. Is the position, then, that sexual freedom has a particularly secularising tendency, that it cuts more sharply than other 'transgressions' across the hierarchical system? It is certain that, in moralistic theories, hierarchical conceptions are most strikingly applied to sexuality; thus it is demanded that sexual enjoyment be subordinated to reproduction, and the independent pursuit of it is regarded as a grievous sin. In fact, it is especially in regard to sexuality that the conception of sin finds application and that 'guilt' is felt; and it may be that, without exercising some command over the sexual life of the lower orders, authorities could never keep them docile.

Feuerbach, in his *Essence of Christianity*[2] throws some light on this question. He connects Christianity's depreciation of sex with its individualistic character, its concern with personal salvation, and he says (p. 167):

The true Christian not only feels no need of culture, because this is a worldly principle and opposed to feeling [that is, to subjectivity]; he has also no need of (natural) love. God supplies to him the want of culture, and in like manner God supplies to him the want of love, of a wife, of a family. The Christian immediately identifies the species with the individual; hence he strips off the difference of sex as a burdensome, accidental adjunct. Man and woman together first constitute the true man; man and woman together are the existence of the race, for their union is the source of multiplicity, the source of other men. Hence the man who does not deny his manhood, is conscious that he is only a part of a being, which needs another part for the making up of the whole of true humanity. The Christian, on the contrary, in his excessive, transcendental subjectivity, conceives that he is, by himself, a perfect being. But the sexual instinct runs counter to this view; it is in contradiction with his ideal: the Christian must therefore deny this instinct.

Feuerbach, in fact, treats love (natural love) as the core of humanity, the central good; and it may be argued, along these lines, that freedom in love is the condition of other freedoms, that while in itself it does not constitute culture, there can be no culture without it, that it continually enriches and is enriched by the various forms of productive (enterprising) activity —Science, Art, Industry. Thus while, in general, a doctrine of individual salvation is calculated to weaken any *movement* of

---

[2] Trans. Marian Evans, Trübner & Co., 1881.

the enslaved and to nullify or divert their discontent with their place in the earthly system (their 'lot'),[3] the weakening of the fundamental human tie is an important step in the process. It is also, I think, argued by Feuerbach, and it is in any case plausible, that what the religious person sacrifices is something that he values very highly, something that he glorifies by handing it over to divinity. Thus his sacrificed sexuality becomes an attribute of the divine, but, of course, in a distorted, 'idealized' form—and this idealization further serves to keep his actual sexuality apart from the active life which it would fructify. It is, at any rate, not hard to see that the heavenly imaginings of the upholders of chastity are symbolic, that they have a hidden sexual content; there is, indeed, much that is sexual in their manifest content, and one of the commonest forms of 'blasphemy', one of the earliest exercises in freethought, is to explode the mysteries by completing the earthly parallel. There is something of this in *Ulysses* but it is not prominent; the main point for Joyce is the falsity of it all. But that cannot be entirely separated from important social considerations—the central place of sexual repression in any repressive system, the way in which fear of sexuality carries over into fear of social disorder, the linking of chastity (which can never be other than *distorted* sexuality) with quietism.

That Joyce is interested in the question of sexual freedom is shown in his play, *Exiles*, where Richard Rowan 'wounds his soul' in his search for 'freedom from all bonds'. However, the main issue in *Ulysses* is still the intellectual one, and the sexual side of the book is only incidental to that. Even its printing of the 'unprintable' is to be taken mainly as an intellectual rejection of the customary—remembering always that there is a considerable element of sexuality in custom. The most bawdy

[3] Cf. Thamin, *Saint Ambroise* (quoted by Sorel, *Église, Évangile et Socialisme*; appendix to *La Ruine du Monde antique*, Rivière, 1925, p. 309): 'Faisant aimer aux pauvres leur pauvreté, aux humbles leur humilité, il [le christianisme] préparait pour ceux qui veulent avoir leur royaume ici-bas, des sujets dociles et des victimes volontaires.'

conversations (for example, in the Lying-in Hospital) fall far short of what is quite common in everyday life, and are governed by the intellectual and critical interest that character-izes the work as a whole. Moreover, the characters are none of them pronouncedly sexual; Marion Bloom, who has been much referred to in this connection, says a good deal that is not usually recorded (again the attack on the customary), but it is to be remembered that Joyce is giving words to her half-formed and nascent thoughts, and, that being understood, her attitude to sexual enjoyment is not at all abnormal. Her hus-band is more 'perverse', but even his peccadillos are com-monplace enough to those who have given any consideration to sex in society. There is no question, of course, of explaining away the sexual side of *Ulysses*. Sexual entanglements, cross-purposes, dissatisfactions, terrors, are an important feature of the hell of bourgeois existence. But the crux of the matter is servitude and the escape from servitude.

But now it may be asked why, if Joyce's rejection of author-ity is an intellectual one, he does not attack it scientifically instead of artistically, does not write a treatise instead of a novel. One answer is that the artistic attack is more effective. Intellectually, the exponents of hierarchy have not a leg to stand on, but they can *ignore* and promote ignorance. And here the work of science is more ponderous, it demands time and detachment, whereas the work of art is more pointed, it par-ticularizes, and so can bite through the defences of those whom mere argument would leave unaroused. But, again, the antithesis is not so sharp as might appear. The true scientist, who is not devoted to utility, to 'service', produces what may well be called a work of art. And the literary artist, in particu-lar, has much of the scientist in him; he describes, he classifies, he correlates. So when Joyce speaks of 'the eternal affirmation of the spirit of man in literature', he is evoking a spirit which is scientific as well as artistic, and he is specifying what is his own escape from servitude.

It is interesting to observe here that Dedalus refers to what binds him as *history*. 'History is a nightmare from which I am trying to awake.' This awakening is art. Art is not concerned with dates, it is not concerned with the conditions and consequences of its subject-matter, though it may present a succession of phases *within* that subject-matter. Thus, while it may be said to particularize in that it presents something concrete and not a general formula, it may also be said to generalize, to present an 'eternal essence', as Joyce through the medium of a day in Dublin in 1904, presents servitude and the escape from it as states of the human soul. What art, on this showing, is most sharply contrasted with is utility. Utility insists on conditions and consequences; its sharp distinction of means and ends is bound up with hierarchy, with the master-servant relationship. But for art all things are on an equality; they are all alike æsthetic material; in any of them *character* can be discovered. Art, in other words, is concerned not with what things are 'for' or what they are 'by means of' but with what they are. And this is hard to find just because of utility, because in human life things become cluttered up with meanings and purposes. It is this which gives point to the description of the painter as restoring 'the innocence of the eye', breaking up conventional associations; and in the same way the literary artist can be described as restoring the innocence of our sense of humanity, as against adventitious commendations and condemnations. On this basis, too, we can see that the artist is supremely productive or creative—in fundamental opposition to the 'consumer's view'. That is to say, the good artist; for all arts can degenerate, and the bad artist is the supreme purveyor of consolation, the most efficient caterer to the consumptive or servile mentality.

Taking art, however, as good art, we find it diametrically opposed to preceptual morality; and what Joyce has shown us in *Ulysses* is the crisis in the struggle of a soul from bondage to freedom, from moral compromise to artistic integrity. It is thus a very special product; like all Joyce's larger works it is an essay in the theory of art as well as in art itself. It not merely does what art does but shows what art does; and, being thus a double attack on moralism, it is doubly attacked by the moralists. But, leaving this special case and taking art in general, we can say that it breaks the rules, transgresses boundaries, that is, the rules and boundaries set up by human purposes; it follows the lines of the things themselves. In so doing it is dangerous as well as revealing; it stimulates new perceptions, but it runs foul of the safety system to which men cling. At the same time, such a system is never actually safe; safety or crowd motives (characteristic of bourgeois mentality) are, as already indicated, liable to panic. Thus the insights of art may often show the way out of a social impasse. When all is said, art occurs in society, in history; *it* has conditions and consequences, however little it may concern itself with such in its material. In brief, the struggle between art and moralism is the struggle between innovation and conservation in society; neither can conquer, but that is not to say that the artistic way of life can compromise (that way lies artistic death and social stagnation); it must still seek to *discover* and to push its discoveries as hard as it can against the inertia of custom and the 'protection' of privilege.

12

Religion in Education

It would be possible to deal with this subject as briefly as with the subject of snakes in Iceland—one could say: 'There is no religion in education.' In other words, education is necessarily secular; the more religious instruction there is in any 'educational' system, the less is it truly educational. But, of course, the position thus dogmatically stated can be supported by argument, and it is to that task that I shall address myself.

The argument to show that religion and education are opposed may, however, be a comparatively simple one. Education may be described as the development of inquiry, the setting up of habits of investigation; and on that understanding religion, in so far as it sets limits to inquiry, is opposed to education. Such limits are in fact involved in the notion of the 'sacred'; to call anything sacred is to say: 'Here inquiry must stop; this is not to be examined.' And, at the same time as religious objects are represented as not to be called in question, they are represented as not open to observation. Here also religion is opposed to education; for if anything is to be learned and understood, it must be subject to observation and experiment—these are the universal educational methods.

To say that anything is accepted by the child as unquestionable or unobservable is to say that it is accepted as dogma or on authority. To accept it at all, of course, he has to interpret it in terms of his own experience, that is, in a secular way; but since he is led to believe that any such interpretation is unjustified, he is left in a state of bewilderment and has to nurse his fantasies in secret. The Freudians, for example, think that the parental figures (particularly the father), as recollected from infancy, supply the real content of the child's religious conceptions; but this (admitting it to be a natural interpretation and leaving aside the question whether it is universal or not) is certainly not a position that the religiously trained child would be permitted to maintain. And since his natural inquiries are thus impeded, since he is frustrated in his endeavours to bring religious dogma within the scope of his understanding, his educable capacity is necessarily lowered.

The point can be further illustrated from the child's response to the assertion that God made everything . . . 'But who made God?' In asking this question the child is proceeding sensibly; he is using the conception of 'making', to which he can give a meaning in terms of his own experience, in order to bring the conception of God within his grasp. But when he is told that God is uncreated, that is something which he cannot bring to the same test: it is something avowedly above his understanding, and to try to make him accept it is to make a direct attack on his commonsense. And the same applies to religious dogmas in general; either the child interprets them in terms of his own experience and so secularizes them, or he accepts them in a confused manner and has his understanding weakened. His mind is divided, his inquiries into the connections of things are blocked at the outset, if he has to draw a line between sacred and secular events or between the spiritually true and the literally or materially true.

Such teaching has a bad effect on his education in general; it tends to make him either cynical, giving verbal adherence to doctrines in which he does not believe, or credulous, believing what he is told, accepting conclusions without developing the power to follow out a line of inquiry. For it is quite impossible to restrict his inquiries in one direction and leave him as capable as before of inquiring in other directions; religious dogma itself must employ secular material, and thus credulity, the acceptance of formulae which are not understood, can extend into any field of study. The cynical attitude, the pupil's defensive reaction to the teaching of absurdities, is clearly anti-educational in its tendency; but credulity is without doubt the greater evil—and few, even of the cynical, escape it altogether. Whatever may be the variation in types of response, the general effect is to prevent the child from becoming a solid and critical thinker.

My exposition so far can be summed up in this—that to say that any subject-matter is open to investigation is to say that it is secular; to say that it is not secular is to say that it is not open to investigation and hence to understanding. What I should further contend is that with the evil of unintelligibility is bound up the evil of authority, that the inculcation of dogma carries with it the imposition of certain forms of behaviour. It will scarcely be denied that 'sacredness' and authority go together; but the orthodox would contend that the authority they uphold is a supernatural or superhuman one. I should argue, on the contrary, that we are invariably brought back to a *human* authority, that it is some set of human claims that religious teaching sustains.

In the first place, as we have seen, unless the child is acquainted with God as a concrete and observable being, he can attach no precise meaning to the assertion 'God has authority over you'—at most, it means that *there is* an authority over him. But, in so far as he accepts this, he has to fill it out with some of the actual material of his experience—and he does so with the figures of his religious preceptors, those who come to him as the *agents* of divinity. That, at least, is his first position, but, of course, he carries his recognition of authority much further. This is where the political usefulness of religious teaching comes in; the credulity and submissiveness it engenders carry over into other spheres and promote obedience to secular authorities. And for this political purpose it is better that the doctrines accepted should have a considerable degree of unintelligibility; more room is left for the operation of fears and less for the counteracting influence of knowledge. The dogmatism and mystery-mongering here in question are exemplified also in 'dialectical materialism' and make it a very suitable instrument for inducing submission to the ruling order in Russia.

There is no doubt that this, in the main, is how the child takes religious teaching; he thinks of God as a policeman he cannot dodge, one who will be aware of his transgressions even if they are concealed from authorities closer at hand and who has the power of inflicting particularly severe penalties. But, while it is reinforced by such fears, the actual authority is always human; and criticism, in removing its religious cover, at the same time reveals its arbitrary character. We may be told that the author of all things wants us to act in this or that way, for example, to be chaste. But how can it be proved that he prefers chastity to unchastity? His 'representatives' will tell us that the injunction to be chaste is found in his sacred word. But how can they show what word is his, what ways he has of communicating with human beings? The decision must be made quite arbitrarily—just as arbitrarily as it is decided that certain events happening nearly two thousand years ago (I am not here concerned with the question how far the Gospel narratives are historical) give a better clue to the nature of things, are a better embodiment of the ultimate authority, than any other events we like to take. We are always brought back to some human fiat: the authorities to which we are asked to submit are earthly ones.

It should be understood that religious teaching is not the only form of authoritarian teaching in the schools. Patriotic injunctions, in particular, present the child with material of which he cannot have an intellectual grasp. In a system which was directed to the development of inquiry, such matters would be approached gradually and indirectly through the study of history. But when the childish mind, without having gone through such a training, is led unquestioningly to accept certain ceremonies and formulae, its thinking powers are again being impaired. The position can be summed up under the heading of 'discipline'; religious discipline and patriotic discipline are alike alien to education, the discipline of which is essentially that of study itself—intellectual discipline. And this is something that the child acquires by the operation of his natural interests and not by the imposition of authoritative standards. Or, using the broader term 'morality', we can say that the only intelligible morality is a secular one—the upholding of some way of life to which, merely as a fact, we are devoted. Such devotion can, of course, be helped to expression in immature minds, but not by the methods of authority; only by the operation of a similar devotion in the mind of the teacher[1].

If religion, then, were to play a part in education as the development of understanding, it could only be as a *subject* on which various views could be considered by the child and grasped in terms of his own experience. No secularist would deny that religion could be a subject of study in this sense, but, in this sense, it would be a *secular* subject. There would be no question of sacred books or protected doctrines; the subject of study would be religious phenomena (beliefs and practices of human beings) or religion as an element in human culture. But, while this is a proper subject of university study, it would seem to be an exceedingly difficult subject for school-children; and we are not likely to see Higher Religion taking its place alongside Higher Latin and Higher Mathematics at the Leaving Certificate examinations. The same is true of moral theory, which, as a systematic study, is far too hard for children. Nevertheless they can approach these questions, and

---

[1] In connection with 'the discipline of study itself' it is argued that I exaggerate the intellectual element in education, that not all children are fitted for an intellectual training. My answer is that the only alternative to the development of understanding is the development of submissiveness. To be educated, I should say, is to come as fully as possible into possession of the intellectual heritage of mankind. And that means that education is the tackling of *subjects*, not 'the development of personality' or 'learning to be useful to society'—or any other of the loose formulae whereby thinking is discounted.

there is no reason why they should not be acquainted with some of the varieties of religious practice, with opposing religious doctrines and opposing views of the nature of religion, so long as the subject is treated in a secular manner and the pupils are not required to give adherence to a particular creed or to treat any objects as 'sacred'—required, that is, to abandon the attitude of study.

Here we are confronted with the contention that the Christian Church has something special to contribute to education, something that no secular training can give. But while, as before, any view of the world in general or of morals in particular can be grasped by the child only in terms of his own experience (and is thus open to rejection by him), it cannot be said that the Christian Church has made good its claim here; it has not developed any general position worthy of scientific respect or set up any *exact* theory of morals. Indeed, it is largely because the Church has been unable to maintain its standing in society at large, because the morality it upholds has failed to compete with other moralities, that it seeks to maintain a privileged position in the schools.

I would not be understood to be arguing that the morality which prevails in social competition is necessarily the best; but I should argue (1) that the morality natural to an educational system is the morality of education itself, of scholarship, of freedom of thought, (2) that the *protecting* of any morality from competition makes for moral weakness, and (3) that the clergymen who give instruction in schools are not experts in ethical science. Teachers, then, would be well-advised to endeavour to keep the clergy out of the schools. They should very strongly resent the intrusion of ministers who are not trained as educators and who do not approach their subject in an educational manner.[2]

---

[2] It is only, I think, persons opposed to my views on other grounds who have read into these statements an incitement to a violent breach of the law. The words 'to endeavour', which I think I used, do not affect the issue, since physical force may be employed in endeavouring to prevent something just

A number of important problems are raised by the view that, in so far as religion enters into the school curriculum, it should be dealt with by members of the regular teaching staffs. On this subject the *New Statesman and Nation* (in its issue of 17th October, 1942) exercises its well-known talent for obscuring issues. 'We have every sympathy with the view that, where religion is taught in schools, it should be taught only by teachers who believe in it, and not by conscripts who may be atheists or anything they please.' Here by the 'teaching' of religion we are to understand not the treatment of a certain subject but the enforcing of certain conclusions. The writer upholds the right of the irreligious teacher not to have to teach religion but has apparently given no consideration to his right to teach irreligion, that is, to present *his own* view of the matters under investigation—though, if he is a good teacher, he will present it not dogmatically but in such a way as to enable the pupils to develop *their* own views in the light of their general experience.

In fact (as a writer of any political competence would have seen) we are confronted here with the whole question of the rights of teachers in respect of 'controversial' subjects, those, namely, on which there is strong difference of opinion among the public. And I should argue that, if such subjects are not taught controversially, they are not worth teaching, and that,

---

as much as in successfully preventing it. I was appealing to teachers as the possessors of a certain 'professional sense' and suggesting that this sense would lead them to oppose unprofessional instruction and especially to oppose the treatment of any subject not so as to stimulate the critical thinking of the pupils but so as to make them regard certain doctrines as above criticism. Some may think that, as the professional sense of teachers stands at present, my way of putting the matter was pointless; but it should have been perfectly clear that I was taking a long-term view and not imagining that such a policy could be *suddenly* adopted or carried through. However, even if the consideration has no application to this particular case, I would still point out, against the exponents of formal legality, that the amendment of a law has been quite commonly preceded and conditioned by the breaking of it—most particularly, of course, where the law does violence to the sentiments of a considerable section of the population.

if the teacher of history, for example, has not the right to treat the subject in his own way, he does not have professional independence and is so much the less an educator. Dogmatic instruction in *religion* is not the only or the major obstacle to education at the present time, in New South Wales and elsewhere, and any reform on the side of religious teaching would necessarily be accompanied by extensive reforms in the organization of education in general.

Confining our attention, however, to religion in the schools, we may note that this means, as far as British and many other communities are concerned, Christianity in the schools. Now if the teacher is going to deal with this subject so as to advance understanding in his pupils, he should have some knowledge of the defects of Christianity, or at least of the objections that have been brought to it, not merely as involving belief in the supernatural but as a moral position. In my own view, the Christian ethic, as an ethic of renunciation and consolation, as holding out to the lowly on earth the expectation of 'elevation' in some unearthly sense, stands low in the scale of moralities, and I should also argue that the Christian emphasis on the individual and his salvation is inimical to a sound view on social affairs, to an understanding of the achievements of the human mind in science and art, which are essentially co-operative. Whatever view teachers may hold on such issues, it is at least desirable that they should be acquainted with non-Christian ethical doctrines and also with various theories, such as the Freudian and the Marxist, of the nature of religion. This sort of knowledge would provide a valuable background to their teaching even if they considered it impossible, because of the difficulty of the questions involved, to present these doctrines directly to their pupils. It would help them to answer the questions raised by the children who, under conditions where no doctrine was placed above criticism, might get quite a good preliminary notion of the alternative views.

The best approach to religion in education, however, the

one most suited to the general capacities of the children, would be the treatment of religious writings as *literature*. The notion of 'sacredness' would be dispensed with; they would be treated as part of the subject-matter of a system of secular study. Thus the Bible would be considered as a collection of stories that men have told (with no attempt to impose on the children by representing it as the continuous development of a single history or creed), and these would be dealt with like any other stories. J. M. Robertson's view of the Gospels is worth noting here, namely, that they are a collection of dramas on themes of recurring popular interest. This is a view which children could easily comprehend, and a consideration of arguments for and against it need not conflict with the literary character of their general line of study. More generally, the very great influence that the Bible has had on English literature makes some study of it almost imperative in any English course—though it might be argued that its influence on human ideas would also give it considerable relevance to the study of history.

Taking it, as I think we may, that the literary approach is the important one, we are brought on to the further point that the materials for such literary studies should not be drawn solely from Christian sources but should take in, for example, the legends of the Greeks, which have always seemed to me much more interesting than the Christian stories—perhaps because they are connected with the life of a highly cultured people. And to these could be added the legends of many peoples, creation stories, a whole body of folklore as a reservoir upon which the teacher could draw. The essential point would be that such human imaginings and traditions should be divested of any notions of sacredness and authority which would mark them off from other studies. Of course this would mean, for the 'believer', not that religious matters were being approached in a certain way but that religion was being kept out of education. Here I can only reiterate the view for which I have argued, that religion, as belief in something sacred and authoritative, is anti-educational—and those who think otherwise are surely weakening their position if they assert that, unless a child has been brought in early life to treat certain things as sacred, he will never form the conception of 'sacredness' at all.

With all this I would still insist that there are other, and in their general effect more serious, authoritarian influences on education than religion. I have already mentioned unthinking patriotism. There is also the utilitarian outlook fostered in the teaching of science, the uncritical attitude to society embodied in the increasing trend to vocational training. This is where one aspect of religious belief could be of some value, namely, its sense of human limitations as against the cheap 'scientific' optimism which is current. Again, there are valuable features of the Christian ethic, for example, its opposition to revenge-fulness—though this is something about which divines are saying little at present, in spite of the many appeals to revengeful feeling in the press. But such matters are better dealt with in a secular way. There must always be in religious teaching an element of opportunism or compromise, in the attempt to square transcendental imaginings with actual events, and the acceptance of such compromises is bound to hinder straight thinking on the child's part.

To sum up, religion (as contrasted with a preliminary and chiefly literary study of some religious phenomena) can come integrally into education, can appear as a *subject*, only if it is treated as part of the general history of human ideas, as an ingredient in cultural development. This is essentially a study for adults; even if children began it, they could not, at leaving age, have progressed very far. But the encouragement of freedom of thinking and inquiry must inform the whole educational process, and it is to this that religion, as the setting up of the sacred and authoritative, is essentially opposed.

Note

One of the questions asked after my address was whether the type of course I recommended could be given by a teacher who had a specific religious faith or only by an unbeliever. I replied that the teacher who undertook such a course need not be an unbeliever. This may seem to be at variance with my statement that the notion of 'sacredness' would be dispensed with. A brief explanation will, I think, clear up this and several other difficulties.

The point is that, whatever I may regard as the best (the most thoroughly educational) mode of procedure, I do not imagine that it can suddenly occupy the whole educational field. Clearly, if a start were made by including Bible study in English courses and having no separate 'religious instruction', those English teachers (and there must be many) who strongly adhere to Christianity could not help presenting some of their religious views in their lessons. And if I argued that they should be debarred from giving the lessons or commanded to dispense with the notion of 'sacredness', this would be inconsistent with my own ideas of freedom or of what could possibly constitute a 'reform'.

In such courses as I have suggested there would be much less scope for dogmatism than there is at present. But the essential point, the conclusion which I take to follow from my main argument, is that, if once teachers were permitted to express their own views, there would be so much more free communication among teachers and pupils generally that secular ideas would spread rapidly. The enforcing of any method of treating the subject would hinder communication and the spread of secularism. If it were otherwise, if secularism (or, similarly, socialism) could advance only by some sort of prohibition or regimentation, then it would be better that it should not advance. But I believe that it is opposed to compulsion and therefore to compulsion exercised upon Christians, or other religious persons, in particular.

13

The Place of the Academic in Modern Society

The work of the academic, qua academic, is criticism; and, whatever his special field may be, his development of independent views will bring him into conflict with prevailing opinions and customary attitudes in the public arena and not merely among his fellow-professionals.

But this will involve rejection of the notion of the academic's 'place' in society in the sense of his having a particular function within a total social process, his being a particular cog in a general social machine; for it takes no great amount of thinking on social matters, no great acquaintance with the relevant critical literature, to see that no such total social process exists, that it is only in terms of a variety of conflicting movements that an intelligible treatment of social facts can be given.

The totalistic view, which is the view of the uninstructed, has infected a considerable number of university teachers, and is one of the major blemishes in the Murray Report[1] (so warmly received by its expectant beneficiaries), which represents it as an honour to universities to serve 'the community' and shows no sense of the emptiness of this conception as compared with scholarship and investigation, which universities can positively advance. 'The country needs scientists'; and so, however irrelevant this may be to the academic work

[1] Report of the Committee on Australian Universities, 1957.

of advancing *subjects*, and however obvious it may seem that greater assistance would be given to the projected undertakings by a small number of good scientists than by a large number of bad scientists, we must have a multiplication of science students, science teachers, science departments—which will necessarily involve an all-round falling away in quality.

The falling away, of course, is not confined to any one field of university studies; university teachers in general are more and more taking on the character of coaches and ushers, concerned with getting students through ('eliminating wastage', as the phrase goes) and not with *finding out* who is capable of rising, under a certain intellectual stimulus, to a certain intellectual standard—a standard which can only be aped, not attained, by those who have been given 'personal assistance', and shown the methods of passing.

The conception of a university as a business or job also forms part of the stock-in-trade of associations of university teachers. Thus Professor R. H. Thorp (*Sydney Morning Herald*, April 18) speaks of the endeavours of these bodies 'to ensure that academic (sic) salaries keep pace with those in comparable occupations'—whatever kinds of work it may be that are comparable to *thinking*. Such fatuities and such tradesmanlike conceptions are themselves a mark of academic decline, symbolized rather than caused, we may say, by the flourishing of associations of university teachers. The unimpressive list Professor Thorp gives of matters other than salaries in which staff associations have taken an interest includes the proposal to have 'a regular universities conference to discuss academic problems' ('if we all get together and talk, something is sure to emerge' appears to be the principle here) but makes no reference to the Orr case,[2] which has been handled by Australian staffs in a pusillanimous and incompetent way, and to which they gave even lukewarm attention

[2] For a discussion of this case see W. H. C. Eddy, *Orr*, Jacaranda Press, Brisbane, 1961.

only after the Tasmanian Presbytery shamed them into making some show of investigation.

Professor Thorp speaks as if anything appertaining to the university (or, perhaps, to the teaching staff) were automatically academic. Now it may be conceded that it is universities that give the greatest stimulus to systematic thinking and that what, outside of them, is represented as of this character is most commonly crankery. But we have to take a pluralist view of the university as well as of society in general and to see that, within any so-called academic institution, there are non-academic and anti-academic activities—that what is academic (for it is a question of movements and traditions, and not of 'individuals') has to fight for survival against pseudo-academic 'philistinism' as well as against the incult social mass, that the struggle of culture against 'bourgeois society' exists also on the campus.

This has always been the case; but the academic had more of a fighting chance when any member of staff might be assumed to have had a liberal education in which he acquired some knowledge of the classics of literature and philosophy. The absence of that condition today explains the absence of any distinctive and recognized academic view on public affairs; its place is taken by the naive and unlettered views which emanate not merely from scientists but from psychologists and educationists. It would be especially on *education* that strong academic pronouncements would be looked for, but the baleful influence of 'the new education' has ensured that university spokesmen are commonly as devoted to philanthropy, as concerned with aids to careers, as the most ignorant outsider. In view of all this it could almost be said (although critical voices are still raised here and there) that the place of the *academic* in modern society is nowhere. At any rate, while it may be of interest to consider how the academic spirit will, where it survives, express itself, it is clear that the voices that speak in the name of universities are, for the most part, far from academic.

It is, then, the first condition of critical thinking to take the pluralist line, to reject the *unitary* conception of universities as of society, to see that they can exhibit intellectual force and uphold culture only through the operation of a vigorous opposition—an opposition to officialdom and legalism, to the *pretence* at unity and the claim to speak in its name. Such opposition, however, has been greatly weakened by the growing unwieldiness of universities; more and more is done by official fiat, and less and less by regular academic processes of discussion and recommendation—many professed academics, indeed, being impatient of discussion and favourable to bureaucratic short-cuts. This is what Professor Orr understood in the Tasmanian struggle, and what the mainland staffs have signally failed to comprehend in the Orr case and in their own situations. They do not see that it is the business of a professor to be a 'trouble-maker' in the sense of one who continually raises critical questions, that he is hampered in his *academic* work if he cannot put forward criticisms of university government and administration—and not at all *advanced* in that work by concerning himself with 'determining university salaries on a nation-wide basis' (in Professor Thorp's fine phrase). They do not see that they have badly let down the Tasmanian Royal Commission, whose proposals, aiming at academic autonomy, were at the opposite pole from the establishment of a *servant* status for university teachers.

There can, of course, be no thorough-going academic autonomy so long as non-academic 'governing bodies' exist, but those who are realistic enough to see that such bodies cannot be abolished overnight should also be able to see that academics must maintain continual opposition and criticism. It is the condition of the possession of any academic character by universities that the teaching staff (more properly, the thinking staff) should not be subservient to any body which is without competence in the subjects to be taught or, for that matter, in methods of teaching and examining. The general notion of supervisory bodies which mediate (or act as a buffer)

between unworldly thinkers and 'the world' may have something to be said for it. But it is inevitable that what has the
status of a governing body will in some degree interfere with
the academic process, will impose its own worldliness on
academics. (A comparable case is the Sydney University
Chancellor's application of the notion of 'good taste'—that is,
the acceptance of conventional 'down-town' standards—to
attempts by *students* to break new ground on public questions.)
This interference especially takes the form of the imposing of a
professional view, the treatment of the university as 'training
for the professions', as having its objects outside itself—so
that, for example, we have the B.M.A. or 'the judges' represented as having views that the university must take account of
in determining the range and content of its courses.

Thus, leaving aside such enormities as the administration's
keeping the staff under personal surveillance or taking seriously the accusations of any informer who comes along, we
must recognize the inevitable clash of views of the nature of
the university and the need felt by academics to uphold its *inner*
life and to deny the right of non-academics (whatever their
official position) to speak in its name. From this point of view,
Orr fulfilled the requirements of an academic position
immensely better than the mass of Australian 'academics',
who have shown themselves to be either philistines, ready to
accept the tradesman's role of training for the professions, or
conventional ditherers, trying to make the best of both
worlds, having faith in the joint service of learning and of
'public interests', in the combination of academic freedom
with government by worldlings—and resenting Orr's breaking through the reconciliatory pretences. They protect themselves from the accusation of servility toward established
interests by plaintive demands for evidence—(Can we be
assured of this? Can that be disproved?) and thus blind themselves not only to the complete absence of evidence against
Orr, but to the importance of his stand for academicism. Here,
as in other cases, the middle-of-the-road merchants are even

more influential than the stubborn 'reactionaries' in preventing either the taking of any decisive action or the formulation of any clear conception of the academic position.

One of the main factors affecting the attitude of Australian university staffs is their fear of the law. But, whatever the legal position may formally be, no genuine academic will ever admit that the academic process is really governed by the nominal governing body or that it is really administered (directed or 'run') by the administration.

Neither of these organs is in the least degree capable of *giving an academic character* to an institution of higher learning, and therefore neither will command the *obedience* of academics but both will be met by regular academic criticism and opposition. It was clearly the intention of the Tasmanian Royal Commission that, if its recommendations were adopted, the staff would be the authority on all 'academic' matters. Apart from all dispute as to what these are, there is never, in the case of any such division of powers, any settled equilibrium but there is a constant struggle over lines of demarcation. The case of Tasmania has shown how close a staff can be brought to powerlessness; but it can never be absolutely powerless, or teaching and inquiry could not go on.

And, in so far as there is an active academic body in any university, it will strive constantly for a better position, for greater academic autonomy. It must be admitted that Councils, Senates, etc., in these parts are peculiarly distant from any conception of things academic; but wherever there is an institution of 'higher education' there will be a similar division of powers, a similar struggle between worldliness and unworldliness, between learning and utility or business.

The position is the same with regard to legality in general. Here, also, the question is of adjustment among competing interests, of a division of powers varying from time to time, with no fixed position which is 'justice'. The Orr case has exposed university staffs as having no sense of the limitations of law, of its rough-and-ready character, its lack of scientific exactness—and of the fact that this inexactness cannot give a special expertness to legal functionaries, who have no specific field of knowledge, but follow custom in their adjustments of disputes, while professing to give definitive solutions, to give us something positive and socially indispensable in 'the rule of law'. Few take so crass a view as do those who speak as 'the University of Tasmania' and profess to take Court decisions as the supreme guide in the moral field. But equally few appear to recognize that it is particular forms of social activity that furnish the positive content of morality, and that neither law nor 'The State' can operate except as adjusting their differences, that neither can positively direct or instruct them.

Here, indeed, we find the meaning of the much-canvassed 'academic freedom'. It does *not* mean that academics have the same rights, the same standing 'before the law', as any other citizens; it means that they have a special province, a field in which they can say: '*We* are the experts here; *we* can tell you (the Law, the State) what has force, what *runs*, in this department of social activity.' This is the position with regard to literature, the censors of which can be condemned by academics as ignorant of literary principles—over and above the general condemnation of paternalism, of the State's professing to be able to give positive moral instruction, when in fact questions of morals are questions of spontaneity or originality and not of the imposition of fiats. In general, in so far as the State or the Law claims a *total* and not a *marginal* function in social affairs, it can only meet with the strenuous resistance of academics, wherever they may be.

How far Australian university staffs as a body are from this standpoint of opposition, of independent thinking, is shown by their complete unwillingness to criticize the working of legal institutions and to stand out against university organization 'as by law established'.

They have in fact accepted the status of servants (making no protest, for example, against the 'right of summary dismissal'), and their main concern has been the obtaining of better terms from their masters. It is hard to conceive any greater alienation from academicism than now prevails—though no doubt even that is possible. At any rate, the place of staffs of this character (paid trainers) in modern society is certainly not the place of academics. That name cannot be applied to a mass of conventionalists who have much more notion of personal position than of objective thinking.

It will still be a main part of the work of those in whom the academic spirit survives (it will be a condition of their proceeding with criticism in any field) to 'scourge the errors of the age', to act as *critics* of modern society, to attack modernist ideology in the form of 'the fresh start', the re-making of the social fabric—as against simple adherence to the cause of learning, to the continuity of culture. In attacking the linked notions of 'welfare', progress and equality, the academic as social critic is attacking the false conception of the State as a directing ethical force (or of 'welfare', the receipt of economic goods, as *standing above* the ethical goodness of original thought and activity) and the no less false conception of universal educability, which, in its process of levelling down, is destroying intellectual distinction and thus destroying education. It is only as *standing for* distinction (the distinction, in particular, of what is academic from what is not) that the academic can have any place in society, any social role. To counteract egalitarian ideology, to uphold enterprise and originality against it, is certainly a tremendous task—not least in universities, on which 'modern ideas' are gaining a steadily stronger grip, as is illustrated in the helplessness, the lack of criticism, with which our 'academics' have confronted the Orr case. But, even if this is a particularly evil age, opposition has been the task of genuine academics in all ages; and some encouragement may be drawn from the signs of shakiness that exponents of 'the trend of the times' still exhibit in the face of such opposition as occurs.

Index

This index covers only the ESSAYS ON EDUCATION by John Anderson himself; it does not cover the INTRODUCTORY ESSAYS.

228 INDEX